THE ART OF STAYING SANE

The ART of
STAYING SANE

By
JOSEPH BARTH

Foreword by
PIERRE VAN PAASSEN

Essay Index Reprint Series

 BOOKS FOR LIBRARIES PRESS
FREEPORT, NEW YORK

INTERNATIONAL STANDARD BOOK NUMBER:

0-8369-1783-9

LIBRARY OF CONGRESS CATALOG CARD NUMBER:

70-117757

PRINTED IN THE UNITED STATES OF AMERICA

FOREWORD

The fact that exceptionally able young men who could, if they chose to do so, easily make a mark on their time in another sphere of life, but who nevertheless prefer to enter the Christian ministry with all its arduous, soul-trying vexations, frustrations and poverty, was a source of constant amazement and mystery to me until I became acquainted with Joseph Barth, the Unitarian minister of Miami, who is the author of this book. Barth's word and work revealed the secret and unraveled the puzzle. Barth was driven into the ministry by a power stronger than himself. An all-compelling zeal for justice, a strong idealism and a passion for the truth were and are the motive power behind his choice of vocation. In other words, in his case it is the Creator Spiritus operating and making decisions.

Joseph Barth, *"our* Barth," I would call him, has the prophetic spirit as few have it in our day. This book of sermons shows that he can be very patient, but that he can also be angry with a quiet and self-possessed intensity. The sight of injustice, of strength or wealth presuming on its advantages, of insolence in high places, calls out in him something like the passion that has made men patriots when their people were oppressed, something of that temper which will always make tyranny insecure, and persecution hazardous.

With it all, and perhaps chiefly, he is moved by an immense love for his fellow men whom he sees in that light in which Jesus saw them when the Master was innerly moved with compassion: as straying sheep without a shepherd. He writes as he speaks, to the point, and in the language of our time. These sermons are comparatively short, but they are exceedingly plain. They are free from rhetorical ornament as well as from all forms of pedantry and affectation. Barth is perfectly capable of holding his own before a learned body, but in the pulpit he never allows his sermons to degenerate into mere generalities. By this I do not wish to infer that the bundle which follows here is lacking in literary merit. Its simplicity of language is indeed the mark of its genuineness.

The cause of liberalism in religion, which, in the final analysis, is the cause of human freedom, is not lost as long as we have men like Barth teaching us and speaking without fear or favor. Always and everywhere there have cropped up independent spirits who resist the encroachments on human liberty. No age has been so barbaric, nor has any tyranny been so systematic but that there have been found individuals willing and able to evade and to confound the arrogance of majorities and to defend the truth against the monomaniacs of power. Joseph Barth is one of these spirits, and this, his first book of sermons, furnishes abundant proof of it.

Therefore: Nihil Obstat!

Imprimatur!

PIERRE VAN PAASSEN

CONTENTS

THE ART OF STAYING SANE

I

THE ART OF STAYING SANE

Not long ago I was thumbing my way through the nineteenth volume of the Encyclopedia Britannica looking for "sanity"; ro—Roman Catholic; ru— Russia; sa—safety glass; St.—St. Asaph; sal— Salamander; sam—Samson; well, where was "sanity"? Ah — san — San Antonio, and then Sand, George; Sandburg, Carl; and now we're getting close, sani — "sanitation." The next flip of the pages landed me in the middle of "sanskrit" which is plainly going too far if you are looking for "sanity." So I went back to "sanitation" and eased over a single page toward "sanity." But then imagine my surprise when I discovered that between "sanitation" with its sub-heads of baths, showers, urinals, lavatories and kitchen sinks, and the next heading "San Jose" there is no sanity and look as I might in volume nineteen from Rayn to Sarr, I couldn't find "sanity." Imagine it! In the greatest popular encyclopedia in the world there is no "sanity." Think I to myself, "I will have to write Robert Maynard Hutchins a letter of protest."

Disappointed and disgusted, I turned to volume fourteen (Libr to Mary) and looked for "lunacy". Ah — there is was in black, bold type in the center of the page: LUNACY, but under "lunacy" there was no treatment of the subject, only a note, "see insanity." So—I start out looking for "sanity" and I wind up somewhere between "Hydroz" and "Jerem" in ten pages of "insanity." That kind of thing could happen to anybody.

You may set out with normal good intentions to live thoughtfully, sympathetically, cooperatively, healthfully, responsibly, courageously among your fellows, but unless you are very wise you may find yourself worrying and wondering and fearing and hating and blaming and making yourself ill. Set out to face facts and despite yourself you may end up trying to escape them. Set out seeking sanity and you may end up in some degree of insanity.

The difficulty goes much deeper than merely wanting to be sane. Everybody wants to do what he believes to be right. But as Socrates pointed out, a person of good will without intelligence may cause just as much social evil as the person who lacks good will. Staying sane is much more complicated than merely wanting to stay sane.

A sane person is a responsible person. A person who is thoroughly responsible is first of all one who recognizes the necessity of finding real correspondence between words and ideas in the mind and the inner or outer world those words and ideas are supposed to describe. It is irresponsible to shout out the word "fire" in a crowded theatre if there are no actual threatening flames or billowing smoke trails to justify the speaking of that word. The words and the ideas in our heads and on the tips of our tongues should stand for something real in the world about us. If the word "truth" has any validity amongst us it ought to be because that word stands for a causal

relationship between things and ideas of things, between reality and words.

Sanity begins, therefore, in straight, descriptive
thinking cultivated amongst us by a clear communication of that thinking in accurate word symbols.
"Greatèr love hath no man than this, that a man lay
down his life for his friends." There is a responsible,
a sane description of a high kind of "love." The man
who wrote it knew a reality that corresponded with
his idea. It is a clear description and you reading it
don't need to drive yourself half crazy trying to
understand what its author meant by love.

But sanity consists of much more than the responsibility of relating words and ideas to specific aspects
of reality. The word sanity also refers to our responsible actions toward people. If within the limits
of our ability and according to our convictions, we
hold ourselves responsible for the life, growth, maturity and creative joy of other people, then we are
sane. Yelling "fire" in a crowded theatre, even when
the hot flames are shooting out from the stage back-
drop, may not be the sane thing to do. It may be
truthful description, but yelling that description may
be a crazy thing to do. It may be such bad judgment
as to amount to gross irresponsibility. The whole
truth in all its startling, shocking implication may not
be the thing to yell from the housetops in every
situation if you are interested in the life, growth,
maturity and creative growth of your fellows. There
is a responsible way and there is an irresponsible way
of using even the truth.

If we want to practice sanity, we do owe reverence
to the truth but we owe reverence to people also and

we must combine those twin reverences in thought and action if we want to stay sane. Now if you think that a difficult task in real life you are quite right, but your test in trying to stay sane has really only begun to reveal its complications. Did you read the tragic story of Henry Lamont Cooper and his mother as it appeared under a January 3, 1947 dateline in a local newspaper? The headline said, "Man Lives Thirty-nine Years as a Baby." According to the account, a mother in Salford, England, could not bear to have her son face the hard facts of life, and so for the thirty-nine years of his life, she dressed him as a baby, fed him with a spoon, kept him in the kitchen behind barred and curtained windows, allowed him to speak to no other person and spoke to him only in baby talk. Then one day the neighbors noticed that the milk was not being taken from the steps of the home and they went into the house to investigate. They found the mother dead and the thirty-nine-year-old baby cowering in the corner afraid of them. They took the son to an institution for care and buried the mother. Nine weeks later the thirty-nine-year-old baby died and was buried in sight of his mother's new grave. Said the doctors: "The son was normal physically and except for the misdirected love of the mother, might have been a normal person."

"Except for the misdirected love" he "might have been." That, of course, is an extreme case of "momism" about which you can read some vitriolic accounts in Philip Wylie's *Generation of Vipers*. But from a psychoanalytical point of view and indeed from a moral point of view, it is not as extreme as it sounds.

In fact, from these latter ways of reviewing it, the story is more typical of us all than it is unusual. Giving food to a youngster of ten with a spoon is unusual; feeding a person of thirty-nine that way is extraordinary. Covering a thirty-nine-year-old body with baby-dress is astoundingly infrequent. But what of spoonfeeding the mind or baby-clothing the moral will? Is a spoonfed mind unusual in our nation? I'm a Catholic because my parents taught me; a Unitarian because my father was one; a Democrat because I live in the south, a Republican because of Uncle Charlie!

And why do you "feel good" in silk and "cheap" in calico? And why do you feel that a man who steals should be "punished"? Why are "planes more dangerous than automobiles"? Why is Franco a "Christian gentleman" if you go to confession and a skunk if you go to a mass meeting in Madison Square Garden? Why is New York the greatest state to New Yorkers and Georgia the best state — even with Talmadge — to Georgians? Why don't Americans fight in the German army and Rumanians in the American and Germans in the Russian? Why do not the Christians join Buddha in their mystic trances or the Buddhists have their ecstatic sense of being joined with Christ? Why are Mom and Pop better than anybody else, even if they are worse than most anybody else? And why is it that in a backyard children's scrap, "our children" are generally right even when they are wrong? Why "secret treaties," "father knows best," "let Congress handle it"?

The fact is that all of us are victims of our parents and teachers, of our traditions and conventions. We all have spoonfed minds and baby-dressed wills and none of us can look squarely at all the facts because, before we began to look at facts or for the truth, blinders were put on us, rose-colored glasses, and we tend to see reality through the eyes of our babyhood conditionings; that is, through spoonfed minds! Our personalities, our habits, our temperaments, our wills, are a product of a process which most of us have never examined because most of us have never stopped to realize it exists.

A baby of thirty-nine years died because of misdirected mother love. She "meant well" but what did she do? All our parents meant well and they were the victims of their parents, who also meant well. What did they do? Why, unless they were very unusual, they victimized us without even knowing that they themselves were victims of a system of unthinking indoctrination which has been going on for centuries.

Look at patriotism in these days. We all feel it and our patriotic fervor leads us to approve the killing and the threat of death in the killing of thousands, yes, millions of young and old human lives. Are you being sane when you approve and pay for the suicide of the race. Were the Germans sane? They weren't. Of course they weren't. "They started it." Of course they did. We all know they did. We are thinking close to all the facts of history when we say it. We were "forced into war." We "don't believe in war." We "had to do it." There was "no alternative." We must "accept our fate and live." "Hitler is crazy." "Hitler must be stopped." Are you interested in facts, in sanity? Would it interest you to know that I have just given you almost word for word, Hitler's reasons, excuses and rationalizations for going to war? Dig out his speeches and you can read them all. Our reasons are the same as his, and he was as sincere when he made them as I was when I made them, and as sane as you were when you made them! And he meant as well for his people as we mean for ours.

Mother always means well and so does father and so did Roosevelt and so did Hitler and so do we all. But mother spoonfed Henry Cooper and dressed him in baby clothes, and because he couldn't adjust to the swiftly changing world he found himself in at the age of thirty-nine, he died. Why do you think that fifty million people have died of violence or starvation in the last five years? Was it because they thought factually, and in terms of the social welfare, responsibly, toward all their fellows in the real world we all live in together? No, by the God of Truth, it wasn't for that reason that fifty million died and another fifty million still suffer. They died, or they still suffer, because they were so fed provincial, baby food prejudices that they could not even see the real facts of the really interrelated world we now live in. Being unable to deal with the harsh facts of the great world they couldn't even squarely see because of their prejudices, they had a violent nervous breakdown the name of which was global war. They had? We had! We are part and parcel of that war fact. We could find no more socially creative answer. We could find no superior will.

Why listen! We say we are a "Christian civilization." If Christianity teaches anything it teaches that we ought to have regard for our brethren under every star. Who is your brother? Remember the two thousand year-old story of the good Samaritan? Why the man across the street, across the tracks, across the state, across the nation, across the world — is your brother. And what did our Christian civilization do to those young men who wanted to have enough regard for those of other nations not to set out to kill them? Why in Germany, it shot them, and in the United States, it put them in concentration "work camps". "They were crazy," those conscientious objectors. They didn't face their responsibility in war time. "They deserved to be shot." There is logic in it. But is the logic sanity or insanity? I have heard many Americans say that kind of thing: "Shoot the crazy CO's." And shoot them is exactly what Hitler did; but Hitler was, as we all know, stark mad.

Well, who precisely is insane? Two possible answers seem to me to stand out clearly. First, that person is "insane" who will not responsibly reinforce all that our well-intended parents taught us to believe right, lawful and true. That is one answer. It is certainly the answer that conservative society tries legally and propagandistically to enforce. It is the answer society gave to Socrates as it demanded he drink the hemlock. It is the answer society gave when it judged Jesus a criminal and hung him on a cross. It is the answer which put Eugene Debs in jail in the last war and the CO's in refined concentration camps in this war.

The second answer is this: that person is sane who, despite the conditioning of well-intentioned parents, teachers and conservative society, seeks in himself to understand how and why he has been taught to believe as he has, analyzes his own thought processes and emotional reactions or asks somebody else to help him do it. And then having critically understood his own mind-sets, his own reaction patterns, his own prejudices, sets out in good earnest to discover with fresh, scientific eyes what he himself and the universe he lives in is really like and what his responsibilities are to himself and to his fellows and to it. Now, while it is a good thing to know that most people, including those who wrote the Encyclopedia Britannica and those who administer the law, judge sanity or insanity by the first answer, I doubt whether you can stay very sane trying to practice it. The fact that two-thirds of the people of this country will sometime in their lives be at least minor neurotics is almost proof of the folly of the practice. There are, at the moment, as many people in the country who are in institutions which care for more-or-less crazy people as there are people in colleges and universities!

I shudder at that thought and try to reassure myself that there is a better way of discovering wisdom and avoiding gross neuroticism than by simple, irresponsible worship of provincial *status quo;* and so I vow to try to practice the second and harder method, hoping it leads me to a resilient adjustment to reality, to sanity. To "know thyself" is the beginning of wisdom, the Greeks said, and so I try to discover who I am and what I am and why I am as I am. More or less at the same time I try to understand the same things about other people and I try also to understand the universe I live in. I try, that is, by all the methods old and new I know about, to earn some kind of sanity, to hold it, to keep it and even to grow in it if I can.

Psychiatry, general semantics, joke books, the Bible, the sacred books of other world religions, the acquaintance with wise men and women, the one hundred best books of the past, glimpses into books that may be considered the best books of tomorrow, modern science and its findings, periods of quiet with myself, arguments with strangers, discussions with friends and relations, forums, sermons and music, drama—these are all ways, I hope, to cultivate sanity. And still I sometimes have doubts about myself. When I write an article or make an address or deliver a sermon and people come to me saying: "how fine" or "how awful," "how intelligent" or "how ignorant," "how cogent" or "how foolish" it is, I sometimes have bad moments. Oh, I like to hear judgments on such things, but I do get a little discouraged at such times. I don't quite know whether to use the first or the second method of judging wisdom or sanity. If you agree in your praise of what I say, how do I know that I am not merely reinforcing your prejudices with my own and so making you "happy"? Or if I provoke hot disagreement in you, am I justified as I'd like to be in thinking that it is "my truth" that has stirred up "your prejudice" to anger? How, in other words, can I be quite sure that I am sane or that you are? Is there a way of knowing that a person is not sane? I think there is such a way. If you find anybody who is absolutely certain that he is sane, then you can be absolutely sure that such a person is dangerously whacky. If you are not so certain about it as a crazy person is, then in all probability there is still hope for you. Then, it is still worth your while to cultivate the sciences and the arts which lead to sanity. The road to sanity leads from self-analysis to understanding of our fellows to a sense of at-homeness in a variegated reality which we will never completely understand. It is an interesting road but it is an endless one with many mysteries along the way. Staying sane is the job, and the fun of traveling on the road is the reward for trying it.

II

HOW TO LOSE YOUR SOUL

FOR SEVERAL YEARS NOW, many self-confessed Christians in our community have been going about worriedly protesting that the Unitarian Church was causing people to lose their souls. I have in the last five years of radio speaking in Miami received many letters from listeners, some timidly, some angrily written, but all assuring me, nonetheless, that I was a bag of nails in the precious tires of the omnibus which should be speeding people on the road to personal salvation.

Four years ago, an amiable and sincere preacher, older than myself, came up to me after a meeting at which I spoke and said: "Young man, if you keep thinking as you did today, you are going to lose your own soul." "Well," I said as I thought for a second, "perhaps you are right." I was going to add: "I hope you are right," when I bit my tongue considering how this statement would be misunderstood and so only hurt the friendly preacher who really wanted to help me. So I didn't say to him as I thought: "I hope I lose my soul!" But today when there is time to explain what I mean, I can say that I hope those people are right who say the Unitarian Church is a place, which, if you come to it, will make you lose your soul. I can reply to some radio critics, who think I am out to see to it that people lose their souls, by saying that I am certainly trying to get people to lose their souls. I can say that I hope I lose my own soul. Right here and now, however, I want to make it plain that the soul I hope to lose is not the same kind of soul my Christian friends are so worried about saving.

To the average Christian, Protestant or Catholic, the soul, which each person is supposed to possess is an amorphous something much like cigarette smoke. It is our spiritual counterpart, they say, shaped like our bodies but without discernible content. And this spiritual or soulful aspect of ourselves is supposed, somehow, to be conscious, capable of survival after our bodies die, and due for an eternal life somewhere, either in heaven or in hell. According to the Christian theory, the job of every person while alive is to see to it that his soul, after death, doesn't waste in eternal hell but on the positive side is saved for eternal bliss. As the practicing Christian says, what doth it profit you if you gain the whole world and lose your own soul? Save your own soul! That is, and always has been the typical and the central slogan of all varieties of Christianity.

Now I can understand—and quite sympathetically —how a person who has no real opportunity for a good life in the here-and-now world, would welcome as good news this theory that he has an eternal soul which may be eternally happy in heaven if he will be blindly faithful to the theory of eternal salvation. I can understand why the underprivileged and hopeless peoples of the world have flocked in to partake of the sacraments as "ways to heaven" or rolled down the revival's sawdust trail, as a prelude to what they believed to be eternal bliss. A promise of any hope to the hopeless makes them pay attention. A promise of eternal bliss to those who live in hells of want, fear, and frustration is indeed welcome good news. Oh yes, I can sympathize with those who crowd into the hot stench of a revivalist tent. I can understand, in a world of many frustrations, why people are avid hearers of the Christian gospel of personal salvation. But to say that I sympathize with the hopeless and understand the frustrated is not nearly the same thing as approving the Christian theory or method of soul saving.

In the old days, which we so like to idealize, when parents had children to the number of ten before they gave the matter a second thought, harassed mothers used to give their somewhat untended and crying youngsters a "sugar-tit" to suck. A sweet morsel no doubt, and as much liked by the youngsters for its taste as it was appreciated by shortsighted parents for its short-run quieting effects. In the long run, however, sucking sugar-tits had drawbacks. Young mouths were misshaped. Doctors said that bad tonsils maybe, and adenoids certainly, and malocclusion no doubt, were the result. Pacifiers might seem fine in the short run but in the long run it was a different matter. I can sympathize with mothers of ten who used them and I can understand the youngsters who lapped them up with gusto, but was it really a good idea?

Is saving your immortal soul a right or a good idea? Personally—and I speak for myself only, as I believe it is your duty to think for yourselves—personally, I think that saving your soul is bad in the long run, in theory and in practice. Take the theory

—hopeful though it may be, to many downcast and frustrated persons. Is there any evidence that we have eternal souls wholly distinct from our bodies and surviving them anywhere after death? I know of no such evidence. There are hopes expressed, there are so-called proofs submitted, there is wishful thinking galore and some flat statements made by people who felt very sure when they made them. But evidences or proofs, there are none. If you have any real proof I wish you'd give it to me. I'd welcome it. Wish-think about it all you like, but don't say you know it is so until you can prove it to the world. About such proof I have not heard. A personally conscious immortal soul surviving the body after death is to me an interesting hypothesis and an old one. But if it is true I have no evidence of it and I have read most of the books. But be the theory true or false, I would be against soul-saving if only because of the evils that accrue from it in practice.

They say that Adam and Eve were thrown out of Eden for wanting to be like God. Well, if getting "saved" is not getting a God-complex I don't know what is. Here we are, a speck of protoplasm on the earth, and our earth lost as a speck in the infinite universe. Our lives are a fleeting instant to a young star which itself flickers but a moment in eternal time. We are a point of consciousness in time and space on earth through no earned victory of our own. We were given our lives as the product of parental love. And how valuable are most of us really? Are we worth what those who sacrifice for us have paid? Are we really worth that much? Then suddenly at the age of fourteen or seventeen or twenty-seven,

up we pop in church, at the behest of some strident
Christian exhorter and discover ourselves the center
of the universe, with God sending his only son just
to garner us in, as sheaves in the heavenly barn. My
—aren't we important! The preacher says so. We
are so important that God has a mansion all roofed
in gold especially built for us, and waiting, waiting,
waiting, if we only will to be saved! Come, drop
those little sins, my friends! Give up the little vices!
Be important! Move into a house on the right side
of the tracks and talk across the back fence with God
for a neighbor. Appealing? Maybe. But what arrogance of wish! What egregious egotism! What egocentric balderdash! No wonder that Hitler and his
kind can take themselves seriously and are taken seriously by ardent followers, when every day dear, little, all-but-hopeless mortals are dreaming a mega-
lomaniac dream of seeing their God "face to face"
on equal terms! If that isn't a God-complex what is?

Mind you I said I can sympathize with and understand those of us little humans who having nothing
and having no hope of anything much in this world
might want to meet God face to face and be bosom-
pals with him in an imagined other world. I can
understand why. But I can't see it as very sane or
very good for those who have their salvation illusion, for those who fail to get saved, or for us who
have to live with them.

And that isn't the worst of concentrating on being
saved for another world. In practice generally,
though one must say there are a few exceptions, the
more you believe in another eternal life beyond this
life, the more important that other life will seem, and

the less important this life and its problems will become. Saving your soul for heaven appeals to people precisely because it takes the cutting edge off the pains of this life. The thought of heaven is indeed an opiate to those who are unhappy in this life. Heaven appeals as an escape from present difficulty and frustration. But an opiate, as an escape, also functions as a sedative to still the active and eager participation of life itself in this life. While you are praying to be saved, while you are holding a revival, while your mind is on heaven, you cannot also be helping with the problems of the here and the now, to make this world a better place. So it is that in so far as you spend your time saving your soul for heaven you are not apt to be contributing usefully to making this earth more humanly habitable. "Saving your soul" may be losing this life.

And now for the worst aspect of soul saving as an end and aim. Jesus, you remember, suggested that we love one another; and you will have to look through a great many sacred books before you find any ethical admonition to self-love. But here as in many other ways the Christian church has preferred to preach its ideas about Jesus as a savior rather than to stick to the teaching of his ethical principles. Jesus said: love one another. That was a central emphasis with him. But Christianity has always taught: save your own soul. If I am any judge, I must say that one of the great troubles with our world is not that Christianity has never been practiced. To the contrary: the great trouble with our world is that this central teaching of Christianity— save your own soul—is everywhere too much prac-

ticed. Everywhere people are scrambling over one
another, trying as they see it, to save their souls, their
skins, their egos. They are thinking primarily about
themselves. They are worrying about themselves.
They are planning for themselves. Christianity is
called, Protestant Christianity especially is called,
the mother of individualism. All right! It was a
good thing for individuals to discover their individ-
uality. It is a good thing for groups of all kinds to
respect individuals. But it is quite another thing for
individuals to come to believe that they are the center
of the universe. And that is what trying to save your
soul does to you. It makes you self-conscious, which
is bad enough for yourself; and after a while it tends
to make you self-centered, which is bad not only for
yourself but for society which has, somehow, still to
live with you. This business of self-centeredness and
self-consciousness has a way of moving in a vicious
circle which at this stage of history is tragic enough
to be appreciated as funny.

Once at a revival I sat in a section on which the
revivalist was concentrating his attention. Finally at
the preacher's persistent pleas two women, each practically entranced, got out of seats near me and started
down the aisle. The preacher welcomed the first dear
sister, but by the time he had her on her knees in
repentance, the second headed back to her seat, obviously in a huff about something. As she seated herself, a friend asked her what the matter was and she
was heard to say in a fairly loud and disgruntled
voice: "Huh! and all the time I thought he was trying to get *me* up there!"

There it is finally: if somebody else gets saved, if

somebody else gets attention it is a matter for jealousy, bitterness and resentment. Myself, I am agreed with modern psychiatrists who say that extreme self-consciousness is one of the great curses of life. In moral terms it could be said that self-centeredness is a great evil. And incidentally, it should be said that it is an evil that is no fun to perpetrate. Indeed, it may be said that those insane persons who are dangerous to themselves and to society alike have only gone to the extreme in self-consciousness and self-centeredness. Yet Christianity has been cultivating this very state, these many years with its age-long admonition: save your soul!

Jesus taught that we should identify ourselves with our fellows in love. The church has tended to teach that we identify God, heaven, and its bliss, with ourselves. Jesus taught that fellowship was heaven and lack of fellowship hell. The church has taught that fellowship on this earth is hell; and lack of fellowship—self-centered salvation seeking—is heaven. Myself, I want none of this churchly soul saving. I am out to lose my soul.

By soul I do not mean a shadowy eternal ghost of my body. I do mean, when I say soul, the reality which is my life. So when I say I want to lose my soul I mean that I want to lose my self-consciousness in an awareness of the life about me. I want, I seek to know the world about me, not as I wish it were but as it is. I want to know people and the problems of persons. I want to give myself for whatever I am worth, be it little or much. I want to give myself in interest, in energy, in concentration, in action, to the larger life, to the larger cause, which is outside myself.

The poet James Stephens describes the process of soul-losing very well. Crisply he asks and answers questions:

> "What is knowing, 'tis to see:
> What is feeling, 'tis to be:
> What is love, but more and more
> To see and be, to be a pour
> And avalanche of being, till
> The being ceases and is still
> For very motion." [1]

There it is! To know, to feel, to love, to act, with such an intensity of concentration on what is outside yourself, that the being—the pitiful little self-conscious being—ceases.

Do you want to lose your souls in joyfulness? Then begin each day with an act of humility. Say to yourself, to your soul: "Look, my little seeking friend! You probably aren't worth too much at best. And if you sit around mooning about yourself, pumping yourself up to airy heavens, you probably will waste your entire life and be worth nothing in the end. You never will know, really, what you were worth. That is God's secret, or mankind's. Open your eyes to them, open your ears to them. Give your attention to them. Understand them, love them, act in this manifold life outside yourself. Now go to it!" And having said so much then betake yourself to life itself. And do as you have instructed yourself.

---

[1] James Stephens, "The Pit of Bliss" *A Poetry Recital*. (New York, 1925), p. 39.

Lose your soul in life. Oh, I don't mean just wine, women and song, though each in its own way might legitimately take a part of your life's interest. I am talking in larger terms. A man is a narrow profligate who throws himself away on these alone. I am suggesting that you lose your soul in an interest in the whole of life. I am suggesting that you buy a book called the *Bible of the World,* which has the sacred ancient literatures of all the world in it. Read it for the contact it will give you with the great minds of ancient days. I suggest you ponder its meanings after a day at business or in the kitchen or after a day at the beach.

Go buy a glass bottomed bucket, get in a small boat, and study the floor and the inhabitants of the sea. Walk out in the dark at night under a star-full purple sky, lie flat on your back and marvel at what you see. Buy a phonograph record, listen to it, then ponder why and what and how you hear it. Try crawling into the skin of the next person you see, black or white, who seems different from you. Imagine living there. What goes on there differently than in you? Study a book of chemistry. Look at a newspaper. Read a poem. Put your nose into a flower. Ponder and perhaps question a suffering face. Ask yourself: "Is my business benefiting the many or the few?" Watch the clouds form in the sky. Suppose you were a snake—or maybe you already feel like one. Then suppose you were a hawk soaring on graceful wing, a sparrow chirping in the snow. What is the hell of modern war really like—and why is it, at all? How does a bee find a flower? What caused

Hitler? and who? Now go back and read something from the great bibles of the world.

Do you see what I mean now by losing your soul? I don't mean frittering it away drinking soda pop or stronger drink. I do mean striving to know, to love, to serve the whole of life without asking constantly, worrying intermittently, "What am I going to get out of it?" I mean knowing, loving, serving, without the slightest bother about saving your soul for a possible heaven. I mean identifying yourself with the whole of life and trying to make some sense —some better sense—out of it than seems to be in it at the moment. I mean thought and feeling and action—directed outside yourself. It means a job for you, an interesting and difficult job, if you accept it. No reward is promised. No goal is assured. The joy and the hell of this kind of life—its rewards and penalties—come, not in what is certainly accomplished, but in what is intelligently, sincerely tried.

From a little blind faith I know you can get the larger promise of saving what is called your immortal soul. My religion prompts me to offer you only the opportunity to lose your life creatively in the larger life about you. My religion prompts me to say of those, who instead of throwing away this life for the empty promise of another, do instead choose to serve this life with their lives:

Lo, blessed are our ears for they have heard;
Yea, blessed are our eyes for they have seen;
Let thunder break on man and beast and bird
And the lightning! It is something to have been![2]

Yes it is something, certainly, to have been. And a little more than something, I suspect it is, to have truly tried to serve the truth and man. It is something to have tried to lose your soul in the larger life of God.

---

[2]G. K. Chesterton, "The Great Minimum," *Modern Religious Verse and Prose,* ed. Frederick Merrifield, (New York, 1925) pp. 377-378.

III

THE GOD I BELIEVE IN

Pink sunrise in a purpling eastern sky;
A day bright with light;
Shadows of approaching twilight;
The dark night.
Stars hide-and-seeking
Behind floating clouds at midnight.
A fat little, round little, noisy little face
Newborn to the world where no face was before.
Hunger pains in the stomach;
Dreams in the night;
In the heart and limbs, a warm yearning
For somebody to love.
Fear gripping the chest;
Loneliness on a high mountain.
The hurricane force of winds
That make a house shudder in the night.
Smooth acres of bay water
Shimmering under morning sun.
Cold hands that once caressed life warmly
And now are stiff in death.

Birth the fact.
Death the fact.
Sensation, thought and life
And the deep need,
The slow gnawing outreach of mind
To understand,
To grow,
To be at home with mystery.

The conception of new life is an ancient joy. Birthing is an old human pain. Seeing, hearing, smelling, tasting, feeling are accustomed traits. Thinking is a traditional effort. Understanding has been a long search. Death is inexorable, a relentless fact.

And the why of it all? The why of it all is clear and certain only to the ignorant and the unimaginative. The miracle of it all is fully understood only by the dogmatic. The answer to the mystery only those blindly conditioned in the simple, credulous ways of our ancestors can give. The ignorant, the unimaginative, the dogmatic, the credulous *know* the answer to the miracles and the mysteries of nature and of human nature only because they are not asking questions. It is not their fault—this lethargy of their minds—which rests in old answers.

Once their minds were eager, questing; but traditional parents and contented grandparents and conservative teachers and orthodox ministers and a conventional society gave to those early out-reachings of inquisitiveness, the slow poison of the ready answer, leaving them with a life which Socrates in Plato's *Apology* says, "is not worth living." "The unexamined life is not worth living," declared Socrates. And his statement throws much light on the conduct of many people, who seem to value life hardly at all because, as I believe, they have hardly examined it at all. They were taught not to examine it, not to question it. And so before they had grown to adulthood, the possible significance of their adult lives was, in great degree, stolen from them. And so it came about that they too learned to answer the old questions with the old answers, almost automatically and became, relatively, automatons of the old faith in an old idea of God.

In the old religions, uncertainty, mystery, miracle, are lost in the·"great certainty" of God. God is the great miracle which explains all miracles. God is the mysterious object of faith which explains all mystery. So, I myself once was taught and so believed. At the age of twelve I was an obnoxious ignoramus who, from reading his larger catechism, *knew* that he knew all the answers to all the mysteries—and knew them "by heart" at that!

I knew that God made me; I knew that God loved me; I knew that God wanted me to be good so that I could come to him in heaven when I died. I knew that he sent his son down here to earth to show me how to be good. I knew fairly exactly, therefore, what being good meant and, on the whole, it was quite simple. I knew where God lived—of course—and I had even been introduced to him in a way in my Bible history book where I saw his picture.

In fact, God had even spoken to me a few times, insignificant country boy that I was, even before the age of twelve. Twice before that age, I recall it distinctly, God spoke to me. Once I played hookey from school to attend an auto race and God told me, in no uncertain terms, that I was committing a sin. And another time, a cousin of mine stole some candy and both he and I had a three-cornered conversation with God about stealing. We both admitted that it was wrong just as the voice of God had told us. But we ate the candy and it didn't make us sick which surprised us, and disturbed us quite a little.

What I have tried to say thus far is simply that we do live in a wonderful and strange reality. But the edge of wonder is taken off it and off our lives because of the twelve year old explanations which most people never question because they have been taught not to question them, but to believe.

But this now I want further to say: believing in God, of itself is no proof that God exists. In fact, a belief in God which is not examined for its truth or falsity is in itself proof only that such a faith is blindly held. I have examined the old beliefs—all of them I could find. And now that I have become a wiser person than I was at twelve, I don't know so much about God as I did then. Of the premise for my faith I think I am surer. And some few facts I think I am more able to relate. But generally speaking, I now feel that there is more to be known about God than all I so far think I know. This at least then has happened to me in searching for God since I was twelve years old: I have grown humble before both God and man. Nowadays, I can keep my mind and heart open to the miracles of earth and sky and life and death. I can be curious and interested and aware and critical and not be stifled as a person because I believe in God.

God, G-O-D—God is a word. One thing we need to understand is that the word itself is only a noise. God is the word the Teutons used to refer to the supreme reality they believed in. Theos was the word the Greeks used; Guth was the word the Goths used; Gud, the Swedish sound; Gott, the German; Deus, the Latin; Dieu, the French. Theos, Guth, Gud,

Gott, Deus, Dieu, God. These are some strange, some familiar sounds. All of them refer to what differing people believed in their day about the reality in which they lived and moved and had their being.

Personally, it makes little difference what noise you make when you want to refer to comprehensive, significant reality. The important thing is not the kind of noise we make, but that we understand alike what that noise refers to. And to what do I refer when I say I believe in "God"? I mean that I need a word that will stand in speech, in a shorthand way, for all reality in which we live and move and have our being. When I want to speak in a hurry about all reality, whatever it is, whenever it is, however it is, for all we know and don't know, I don't want always to have to stop and say all that. Guth or Theos, God or Universe; I want a word, a short word. Can we agree that G-O-D, God, shall be that word? God— in whom we live, and move and have our being.

I am no supernaturalist. I say it to you frankly. If there are any other worlds they are natural worlds related directly to this one and governed by similar, if not identical, principles. This is my faith. I cannot prove it, scientists do not try. They accept it as a working premise of their scientific faith. I accept it for mine. It fits in with what I think I know, but I admit I don't know about "all" reality. Maybe there is no "all" as the human mind would like to think about it. Maybe reality extends forever, forward and backward in process of change in time. Maybe the universe has no boundaries. Maybe God is literally everywhere and everywhere extended to everywhere. I find it difficult to think about, hard to comprehend even by stretching the little imagination that society will allow me to use. But we are fairly certain, in so far as we have a right to trust the sharpened, telescopic eye, that God is grander in space than the bearded giant of my old Bible history book.

"Hundreds of millions of light years" of space may be describing only a sparkle in a cosmic explosion which will radiate through space for ever and forever. Being a space- and time-minded creature, I can at least keep from getting a swelled head thinking I am the center of God's existence when I think about what may be an expanding universe, a growing God.

There is more than one sense in which I think I am not the center of the universe and the apple of God's eye. In times past, thinkers have liked to believe that God guaranteed human values. God, we have said in times past, guarantees the sanctity of life, of our "way of life" and maybe even of our real estate. Of all this I now am rather doubtful. The cosmic process, or God, has so far as I know made no such guarantee to support my ideas in religion, in politics or in economics. The Protestant Church-North, may be a place where Republicans go to pray. But, I doubt if any more Godlike ears than their own hear their prayer. Their own idea of God does, they believe, hear their prayers, but that the universe bends low of a Sunday morning in rapt attention to Republicans-North or Democrats-South to listen and then to set the stars in their courses according to the loudest or the longest prayers—well, that I more than doubt. The God I know is no respecter of persons or of parties, not God as a whole, not the universe entire. I do not believe I live in a moral universe. I do not think I live in an immoral universe. God "as a whole" I believe is neither moral nor immoral, neither good nor bad. GOD IS! God is the groundwork of our lives, the base from which we humans with our human desires argue about our ideas of what is right or wrong, good or bad *for us,* according to our desiring.

God is sun and wind and rain. God is soft breeze which gently kisses us on the sand. God is a hurricane which shakes the windows out of our homes; but whether the soft breeze or the sunlight or the rain or the hurricane is good or bad, depends not on them, but on our desires in relation to any of them. If you wanted sunshine the day it rained, then you are apt to say: "the rain is bad," *as if* it fell on your garden party with malevolent will. If the sun comes out hot on the day you choose for a shady walk, you are apt to say: "isn't this sun terrible?" *as if* the sun had a devil's will to persecute you personally.

But, rain is. Sun is. Wind is. Universe is. Is! With a period after it. And "good" or "bad" are words we use to describe the feeling we have about sun, wind, rain, as they seem to advance or frustrate our private purposes. But God as a whole, or wind, sand or stars which are parts of God's being, are without purpose. Maybe the universe has something better than purpose, I don't know. Purpose is a human idea born of human ability to project wishes as goals to work for.

But all the universe, nor nearly all of God is human; the only human part of God I know is man. Whether humans are comparatively the most complex, most conscious, most purposeful, part of God's life, I do not know. Sometimes I like to flatter myself by thinking so. But I don't know. Perhaps wiser beings than we, more powerful than we, roam the bloodstream of God's reality a hundred billion light years from us. Perhaps there are sensitive beings on Mars who speculate about earth children as we speculate about them.

But that God as a whole, as universe, can set goals as we by our desires are driven "with purpose" to do, that I doubt. God as cosmic purpose I doubt. God as cosmic guarantee of human values, I disbelieve. To argue so, is trying by a mental trick to tie God to the coattails of human desire. That is a human egocentric mania. And while in wisdom we have learned to make our uncertain way on our earth home, we need not fool ourselves into thinking that we thereby control the universe. The universe—God—is the base of life, and as such neither "good" nor "bad," except when with loose and lazy language we charge it with *seeming* malevolence or bless it for *seeming* good will toward our human desires.

Sir Charles Sedley said that "'tis the worshipper that makes the God," and in great degree he does describe how many of our past ideas of God have come into being. Many of our past ideas of God are projections of our own human wishes. We have all too often made our gods in our own image and likeness. And in one sense we must always in some degree do so because we are always inclined to get our own desires, hopes and dreams into our descriptions of reality.

This is legitimate in the sense that we too are parts of reality and our desires are real. But neither we, nor our desires, are the chiefest things, necessarily, about God's universal life. And we but feed ourselves with illusory wish-thinking if we try to make it so. The vast, impersonal, amoral universe outside of man is the groundwork of our human lives from which we are sprung. It is part, and the greater part, so far as I know of God's life. But God has also a personal aspect, a loving aspect, a caring aspect, an aspect of purpose. God's personal aspect consists of persons who may love, care, dislike, seek. God includes us all as nature includes the trees, as the sea includes the fish in the sea. To me, you are persons; to me, in another view of you, you are the personal aspect of God's great life.

At home we frequently say a blessing before meals, "To all the people who have helped us get this food, we are grateful." That is a way we have of stopping for a moment in a busy day to remind ourselves that we humans are members one of another, interrelated in so specific a thing as our food getting. We are members, one with another, of the personal aspect of God's life. We are a part of God, grown to self-consciousness. And while we are smaller than stellar distances, we at the same time are greater than any mere distance because we can measure distance, look through it, and in some degree comprehend it.

I believe in God; the God I believe in is a naturalistically conceived God. The scientist is one who strives with his life to measure, chart, graph, understand, the reality of God whether cosmic or human. The scientist has the ideal of objective description. He wants, if he can, to describe God without letting human desire or human wishes interfere with his description.

The new philosopher of religion will base his thinking on scientific findings. He will submit his philosophical theories to scientific experimentation. The religious theories he develops may indeed go beyond scientific findings, as any hypothesis goes beyond the facts, but they will certainly not claim for themselves a kind of authority that science cannot claim.

The "God I believe in" is nature entire. My independence as a person apart from nature exists in this possibility that I may perhaps be able to choose my own course of action, apart from the conditioning influence of all the rest of nature and of human nature. In so far as I am a free man I can, if I choose, be independent of God. It is possible, I think, for a person to set his individual will against the pervasive way of universal law. It is possible for a person to disregard natural law. You can, if you choose, stand in the way of a tree which is driven by a hurricane; If you like, you can try to stop an avalanche in its drive down the mountain. Personally, I have never thought myself very wise in using my freedom to go against God's natural way of working, whether in the universe or in reaction in my own body. A wiser way seems to be to discover nature's laws and then to work with them, or as some egotists like to put it, to "take advantage" of them. Even the attitude of taking advantage of God through our knowledge has always seemed to me a little out of perspective.

I remember that Margaret Fuller in talking to Thomas Carlyle about nature and her place in it rather glibly and a little deferentially said to him, "Mr. Carlyle, I accept the universe." Said the dour Carlyle, "Gad, you'd better."

I have stood before the parents of a nine-month-old baby, their only son who but a few hours earlier, in a moment of unguarded and completely innocent play, had rolled to the foot of their large double bed and there between the mattress and the metal uprights of the footboard had strangled to death. They believed in a completely personal God and they asked me piteously, "Why did God let it happen?"

I have seen ignorant, greedy, nationalistic people fearful for themselves send the flower of their young manhood off to war to kill and be killed and I have seen them then creep hopefully to church to burn candles before the stone image of their personal God, that they might enjoy the special privilege of having their sons return to them alive. At whose expense, I ask myself, are they willing to enjoy the special privilege from their personal God? How long, I ask myself, shall we go on flouting the laws which govern life and growth and creative joy in this universe and still blame the judgments we bring upon ourselves on a "good God"? Such whimpering ignorance is an insult to the very idea of God. God is the groundwork of justice!—not a dispenser of special privilege or a breaker of natural law.

The God I believe in is not a cruel God, nor yet

a kindly God, nor wise, nor ignorant, nor good, nor
bad, except as people are themselves these things and
use such words. God, the universe, I know is the
base of life, in light of which our desires in action
yield cruel results or kindly, in light of which our
personal goal-seeking results in good or evil for ourselves and our fellows.

Life we were given out of the loins of "Mother
Nature." And growth on the human plane of intelligence and sensitivity and wisdom is our reasonable
expectation in life. Our goal: the better! And creative joy in life is the result of striving for a better in
which to lose our lives for all they are worth. Sick-
ness, worry, fear, hungers unrelieved, jealousy, fighting, and death short of a full life are the negative
results of wrong thinking and wrong action in a universe which is as it is.

God is no judge of men. We are judges of ourselves in God's larger being. There is no guarantee
I can find that the sensitive, personal human aspect
of God's life may not destroy itself, throwing away
its birthright against the avalanche of cosmic power.
Cosmic power, discovered, appropriated, and mis-
used, may be the end of us. I accept the universe. I
accept myself in the universe. I am responsible in
this universe, and Gad, I'd better accept the universe
and myself and my own responsibilities. And so had
you better and so had all humanity else in our own
stupidly destructive death-dealing practices we condemn ourselves to destruction.

If you allow jerry-builders to create a jerry-built
society and you yourself are foolish enough to buy
and live in a jerry-built house, don't blame God if,

when a hurricane comes, you and the town are blown into splintered oblivion.

Wise indeed would it be to study God, as God is; to accept the universe as is. Indeed, if you believe in the God I believe in, you'd better! And you'd better get working on some of your friends to do it also.

IV

THE FACT OF BROTHERHOOD

"ALL THIS IDEALISTIC TALK about the brotherhood of man is a lot of hooey!"

A few months ago I was talking with a college student who would be pleased to hear me call him hard-boiled, and that was what he said. He felt that brotherhood was idealistic nonsense. "Look here!" he said. "You look at the facts of life. The world is at war and we are out to win it from our enemies. The world is composed of 'us' and 'them' and either they lick us, which they won't, or we lick them, which we will! All this brotherhood stuff is just lovey-dovey twaddle."

"But" . . . I started to argue "There are no buts to it," my hard-boiled friend cut in. "The fact is that you preachers can't look the facts in the face. Idealistic. That's what you are. I tell you it's war. Either we or they will go down and brotherhood be damned. In business it is the same thing. Competition is the law. In competition you either sink or swim. Brotherhood! Bah!"

"Well, maybe that's true," I admitted, "but—" "But nothing!" he almost shouted. "You preachers are always trying to find a loophole to escape from the facts." He went on talking excitedly and to report even the gist of what he said, I admit I will have to do just what he said preachers always do. I'll have to idealize his language a little.

In general he thought that the Negro was a savage and will be for at least five hundred years. The Jew was a foreigner who couldn't be Americanized, and a Jap, he felt, was strictly a lower animal, hopeless and fit only for extermination. To tell you the truth, along toward the end of our conversation I was a little afraid that if I said just once more, "yes, but . . ." he would also draw a line between himself and me and prove to his own satisfaction at least, the foolishness of our common brotherhood by tossing me out of his study window.

Fortunately for me, my hard-headed friend is not really as hard-hearted as his talk, and as I went away from his room, although he shook a savagely clinched fist at me, he also burst into a laugh.

Now, I don't know what you may think about such hard-headed criticism of brotherhood. I don't know how your evaluations differ from our friend's superior attitude toward certain groups of people. My own feeling is that at least part of his criticism has a real point. Isn't it a fact for instance that in the tradition of our Judeo-Christian religion we have been told by the church that we should "love our neighbors as ourselves"? And as if that weren't enough, along comes Jesus, the cornerstone of the Christian churches and teaches that we ought not only to love our neighbors but that also we ought to "love our enemies." And isn't it a fact that when we are converted to this Christian religion or when we join the Christian church which teaches these things, that we have at least pretended to try to follow the great commands of Jesus? Haven't the churches and church people claimed in some degree that their churches were actually brotherhoods wherein love to neighbors and love to enemies, even, was to be practiced? Once you are "saved," once you are "converted," once you have "confessed Christ as your savior," once you are a member of the "true faith," once you have "joined the church," then it is claimed you have entered into the churchly brotherhood where love, as interpreted by Jesus, is the rule and therefore are you fit prospects for a heavenly life.

But have the churches within themselves lived as a loving brotherhood? And have they toward outsiders, their considered enemies, practiced brotherly love? In some few instances, yes, maybe. But the rule? Why as a rule they have exploited one another inside the church as much as have pagan outsiders, regardless of their pretensions of brotherly love. Church leaders have demanded tithes of their followers, when their followers had only half enough of anything for a decent life. Priests wearing clothing woven of gold have threatened and cajoled the poverty stricken for an added penny. Clergymen living on the fat of the land have preached love and practiced a class-conscious superiority. Church people, church leaders have indeed in many instances been saints, but in many, many more instances they gouge and splurge and bicker and hate. They contribute to exploitation and wage war in no less a degree than those outside the fold.

And, in so far as the church or the churchmen pretend to the general practice of brotherly love, then my hard-boiled friend is right in calling it "hooey." The fact is for any courageous soul to see, that we do live in a world dominated by bitter, competitive, jealousy and hate. At the moment, hate rules the world, driving great areas of civilization to warring destruction. And if brotherhood means "brotherly love" actually in practice and not pretended or merely preached, then any clearsighted person ought to admit with the hard-boiled critics that brotherhood is an ideal so far off and nebulous as never to be really reached at all. This, I take it, is what the hard-boiled mean when they say that "brotherhood is lovey-dovey twaddle." As an extreme example—preaching love and waging war. Look at this world now. Tell me how much you think the Christian rule of love to neighbors and enemies holds sway in human hearts and minds and deeds. Brotherly love can be, and often is at its worst, nothing but a hypocritical jargon to cover a multitude of exploitative sins. Seen at its best in light of the facts, a loving brotherhood is a far-off, piously expressed ideal.

Now, if brotherly love is, as I believe, but a pious ideal, are we therefore to conclude with the self-styled realists that brotherhood is bunk? Unfortunately most people who granted the "if" in that question would feel that they had to answer "yes" to it. Unfortunately, that is to say, most people who think of brotherhood think it means affection. They would therefore feel that where there is no affection there can be no brotherhood. Or they might say that if there can be brotherhood without affection it isn't important.

It is my conviction however that there is a more fundamental meaning in the word brotherhood, and I think it is very important! According to the myth in the Bible, Cain and Abel were the first brothers on record. They, as I remember it, set out to offer a sacrifice to God each in his own way. And the way of Cain's sacrifice was not acceptable to God. Abel's sacrifice was acceptable. So Cain got jealous and angry about it and murdered his brother. Now, the question is: did Cain's individualistic jealousy and anger, which ended in murder, in any way destroy his brotherhood with Abel? According to the story— and I'm not asking anyone to take it literally—God didn't seem to think that hating or murdering a brother dissolves the brotherly relationship. God's logic in this case seemed to be that once a brother always a brother, once related always related, and if related to, then responsible for!

And God called Cain and he asked him, "Where is your brother?" And Cain being still angry was snippy with God and said: "Am I my brother's keeper?" Cain's irresponsible freshness seemed to rile God somewhat for at that point God apparently struck Cain a blow which sent him reeling down the centuries with a scar on his forehead, a marked man. Cain murdered his brother. He didn't love him. But by virtue of his brotherly relationship, he was held accountable anyhow. Murder, no less than marriage, is an expression of relationship! Brotherhood, then, means two things, more fundamental than love: brotherhood means first of all relationship; secondly, brotherhood means responsibility. And that kind of brotherhood I believe in. That kind of brotherhood is not bunk.

Brotherhood as relationship is not so far away from us as is the ideal. Brotherhood as relationship

is a fact. Put your fingertip on the land area shown
on any globe or map. Suppose you were now suddenly transported to that land your finger touches on
the map. And suppose you were in that land dying
for lack of blood. You might be dying in Iceland or
Japan, in Russia or Siam, in Alabama or Nigeria, in
Australia or in Greenland. The peoples of any of
those places have blood types like your own. The
peoples of those places whatever their religion, whatever their customs, whatever their color could give
you their blood to save your life. That is not an
ideal. That is not pious nonsense. That is a fact.
You are related, and by blood, to all classes and to
all colors of people on earth. You may like that fact,
you may detest that fact, but if you are sensible—
especially if you are really a realist—you will accept
that fact, along with the blood to save your life.

Go to any country in the world among any people;
go as a hale and hearty person. If you are to continue to live you will buy food. That is an expression of relation. You will see and hear and smell
those other people. That is relation. Stay long
enough among those so-called strangers; you will
find friends! Stay longer and their illnesses will
probably visit you. You will "catch" their disease
germs. The germs of the universe are unaware of
the prejudice which makes you think you are essen-
tially different from other peoples. Germs are realists. Germs don't distinguish between Jew and Gen-
tile, between Catholic and Protestant and Hindu, between Negro and white, between men and women.
No—germs are a lot nearer the truth of our common
human relatedness than many superior sounding hu-

mans are. Germs know that "we are members one of another," and they act accordingly. They act on the facts which most people don't know, the facts of human interrelatedness, while we continue to act in considerable degree on the prejudices and illusions of a theoretical, individualistic separation. The humbling truth is that a typhoid germ practices less color, class, racial and religious discrimination than does the average man. Find a loophole in that fact, my hard-boiled friends!

Now I understand why Francis of Assisi liked to preach to the birds, and if some day you should find me happily orating to a garbage pile you will know that I have taken up my ministry among the common unprejudiced germs! They may be scum but they seem to know that "A man's a man for a' that," and they act that way! What glorious consistency!

Brotherhood as relatedness is a fact! I have said that brotherhood to me meant relationship and responsibility. I have tried to give you a few simple illustrations to show that humanity is in very truth physically and spiritually—at this moment—a single related brotherhood. A blood brotherhood! No less! A spiritual brotherhood, indeed! You don't need to yearn for it. You only need to open your eyes and mind to it.

"But," you may ask, "if brotherhood-as-relationship be a fact, why has not religion made people practice brotherly love? It certainly has preached it to them!" I agree that religion has steadily preached brotherly love as an "ought." And I agree that, by and large, what has been steadily preached hasn't been much practiced.

As I see it, people have practiced very little brother love precisely because brotherly love was all that was preached. To tell you the truth, I believe the inventors and manufacturers of the steamboat, the motorcar, the railroad, the airplane and the radio, have done more to get brotherly love really practiced than have all the preachers in all the ages preaching brotherly love. And this is why the preachers have failed and the manufacturers are succeeding. The steamboat, the motorcar, the railroad, the airplane and the radio have as we have used them done two things: they have educated us more than most preachers yet have the courage or intelligence to do, in the fact of our common human relatedness. Travel around the world and you will see that each nation, like our own, has its great and its small, its wise and its ignorant, its good and its evil people. Try to convince a fifteen-year-old youngster who has never been out of Palatka, Florida that there are some Japanese who do not have buck teeth or wear horn-rimmed glasses. For that matter, try it on some people of fifty. They know better. They have seen the cartoons. But send them to Japan; the picture changes.

Our speedy modern methods of communication have let us see more and more clearly that we are, the world around, actually related human beings.

And the second thing modern transportation and communication have done is to bring distant and strange peoples nearer and closer together. First reaction fear! Then acquaintance. Machine transportation makes real relationship conscious. Getting to know strangers is the best way possible to make friends. Get the facts about people and unless you are careful you may learn to love them. Isn't that true about Negroes and whites, about Gentiles and Jews, about "friends" and "enemies"? Many white people in America who want to keep the Negroes in an inferior place know some one or two Negroes for whom they would give their right arms. Many Gentiles say something is the matter with the Jews but they except usually, some few Jewish friends because, as they say, those friends they know are "different." Certainly friends are different. You know them! You trust them, because you know them.

If a preacher tells you you ought to love Rastus George Washington Jones and all his kind you smile up your sleeve at the pious thought, but the admonition won't make you love him or his fellows. Yet, get to know Rastus, get his trust and respect, get to know his mind and his heart, his hopes, his trials, and unless you continue in a careful cultivation of your own prejudices, you may get to be friendly with Rastus. Many a slave in the old days died for his master! Yes, and many a "master" has died for his "slave" despite all talk of superior and inferior peoples. And that's a fact.

Preaching to people that they ought, they ought, they ought, to love their neighbors, regardless of race or color or creed is nonsense. Urging people that they ought, ought, ought, ought, ought, to love their enemies will only get you classed by those to whom you preach as one of the enemies. And that is why preaching brotherly love has failed to make us loving. You can't love what you think you hate. You won't accept your responsibility for your fellow man until you realize the *fact* that you are related to him. Love begins in knowledge and flowers only with understanding. When we realize the fact that we are related, really, vitally, inescapably to all other persons in the world, then we will assume our brotherly responsibility to our fellows, and not before.

When we know in mind and heart that we are, we always have been, and always will be, literally, "members of one another," then we are ready to love our fellows all over the world—and will.

For my part, as a preacher, I dare you, whoever you are, wherever you are, I dare you to select five persons you think to be quite different from yourself; different in religion, in color, in class, in nationality; persons you suspect, fear, hate; I dare you to get to know them. I say nothing of loving; I dare you to get to know all about them, their weaknesses, their hopes, their past lives, their prejudices, their ambitions, I dare you thoroughly to cultivate your knowledge of these five other people without in some degree coming to feel responsible for and with them and even learning to love them, in some degree. Go ahead all you idealists, go ahead you hard-boiled realists, go ahead! I dare you to try yourselves! I dare you to try whether you can really get to know people fully without loving them. I dare all ignorance, I dare all prejudice to try. And as liberals yourselves, striving to change the world into a better place, I dare you to dare others to get to know those they say they distrust, suspect and hate. There is a life project in this for you.

We are a human brotherhood, related and responsible for one another. The tragedy is that most people are ignorant of, blind to, the fact of brotherhood. If you want to live in a better world of brotherly love, then see to it that all people learn the truth of brotherhood as relationship.

V

THE ART OF
NOT DEALING WITH EVIL

PESSIMISTS ANTEDATE DOUGHNUTS by a great many centuries. A long time before doughnuts were invented a great many people saw the hole in them. In our day there seems to be no unusual shortage of those who concentrate on looking at evil to the exclusion of the good. In our day—as usual—there are a great many who see nothing but holes in their doughnuts.

If an Atlantic Charter is enunciated, these dour-minded declare: "Humph! It won't be evoked in the Pacific." If "Four Freedoms" are proclaimed for all the world the pessimists cry: "Oh yeah! There isn't any single place in all the earth where even one freedom really prevails—and now we talk of four freedoms all over the world!" If the Cairo and Teheran Conferences suggest to some people the formation of a really united group of allies, you can depend on it some gloom-puss will pop up to suggest: "You just wait till the war is over and then watch the so-called United Nations blow themselves to pieces with bickering and jealousy!" The pessimist is bound to believe that day by day in every way the world is getting "worser" and "worser."

There is evil in the world and I know it. But there is goodness, too, in life. I know that also. And personally I see no special virtue in dwelling exclusively on the evils. Indeed I see several reasons against such pessimistic procedure. And yet—I find myself frequently wondering in these hectic days whether we would not, all of us, be better off if there were at large in our world a great many more vocal pessimists, who would with stern and bitter language insist that more and more people look squarely at the evils of our world. The reason I say so is because today so many persons are not looking at evil at all.

You and I know, at least in a back corner of our minds, that never before in the history of man has humanity suffered such devastatingly extensive evil as that to which we submitted ourselves in global war. And yet, does the average American know with his heart, does he feel in his bones, the impact of that evil? Are you, as you appreciate the good things in this our life, also facing the evils all about you?

I do not ask that you dwell exclusively on the evil. I do not think you should. I ask merely: do you see the evils as they are? Do you deal with evil as it interferes with the good life? What does your faith teach you about dealing with evil? Or is your religion one which teaches you the art of not dealing with evil?

Let us face a fact. Our own natures tend to make us shy away from evil. When we see an unfriendly or evil person approaching on the street, aren't we apt to want to cross over to the other side and avoid that person? Out driving we try to miss the holes in the street. We avoid situations which might be painful. And even if we have schooled ourselves to face the evil day we tend to put it off. "Tomorrow, or next week, I will pay the garbage tax!" "Next month, I'll see the dentist." We are like that, most of us. We don't like evil. We don't like to face evil. We don't like to deal with evil. We can know, in the top of our hats, that what King Cyrus said was true: "He that spares the wicked injures the good." We can know that for truth; still we must face ourselves and know also that in general we all try to avoid evil. That is the way we are.

Out in Colorado one summer a scout master led his troop up a mountain trail. On the path a rattlesnake appeared. Somewhat disturbed it did not strike. The scout master led his troop around the snake and on up the mountain. But a few moments later the disturbed snake, now carefully coiled, struck out at the next person coming up the trail. The shouts of the bitten man brought the scout master back down the trail to the stricken one, whose life was saved. Said the scout master afterwards: "I'll never again go around an evil."

But most people don't learn as fast as that scout master. Most people skirt the evils, avoid them, close their eyes to them. Most people, that is to say, leave the evils alone to strike in aroused anger at somebody else.

People uncultivated in ethical religion are like that. People undisciplined by a wide social consciousness are like that.

Indeed this kind of human weakness and blindness has a way of expressing itself not only in individuals but in institutions also. Consider government controlled war news as example. When we saw the picture of a bombed and gutted German city, that presumably was good. We saw many such photographs reproduced in the press. But how many pictures of the bombed cities of England did you see in the papers? Such pictures, would presumedly be a view of evil. So official censorship saw to it that we did not see the evil. Like the scout master the government led us around the evil and we didn't even have to look at it, much less deal with it. Let the rattler bite someone else. If we are kept blind to the deed we won't suffer. There it is; the art of not dealing with evil.

I have asked several people in positions of authority why it was that we were shown so few pictures of the rigors and hardships, the horrors of this war. Their answers varied somewhat but all agreed that submitting realistic war pictures to the general public wouldn't be "good taste." The picture of a young American, or of a young Nazi for that matter, with his head in shreds, an arm shot off, and his intestines splattered out on an overturned tank, is "not good taste" to present to men, much less to women and children.

Not "good taste!" And what in God's name is war? Is it a pleasant picnic, then, always to be pictured in splendor and good taste? "Good taste" hides a smashing evil. "Good taste" is frequently only part of the art of not seeing the evil. There is a great deal of such extremely "good taste" practiced in many of our churches right now.

I have a cultivated aesthetic sense myself. I like ardor in restraint. I like music and soft lights. I appreciate the drama of burning candles. Good manners I like. Clean clothes, words spoken truly in quiet, feelings that make themselves felt, a clear eye, talk to the point, dignity of bearing without being stuffed-shirt—all these—are the pleasant securities of civilization. I like these things at home. They are essential in society. They are good in church. Really good taste is a good thing. But "good taste" has become for many—even for many churches—the central vice. "Good taste" has become for many a whited-sepulchre a pleasant disguise for a putrid evil.

Even in Jesus' day the cult of "good taste" seems already to have minced its way into the institution of religion. You remember that Jesus had to defend himself against the criticisms of the cult. "Jesus, you ate with tax gatherers." "Jesus, a religious man, and you took a drink of wine!" "Jesus, you talked with prostitutes!" "Jesus, you had friends who were ordinary common laborers. And, you got angry once at those accommodating money changers in the temple!" Tut! Tut! Jesus! You should have better taste. Certainly it is a lucky thing you don't have to preach in most churches these days. If you started talking about the plight of the common man in Spain or Peru or Poland, like as not the good-tasters would condemn you as being against organized religion, as maybe you'd have to be. You wouldn't have to associate with the common man, just talk about his conditions in the pulpit. That's all you need to do nowadays to be in bad taste. "Good taste" is "better" in our day than it was in yours. You appreciate the joke, Jesus. I thought you would. And as for prostitutes—why we don't even mention that word in most churches, well, hardly ever, in church or out. You see it isn't "good taste" to see such facts anymore. We have "progressed" in the art of not dealing with evil. Our churches have "progressed."

What do you think would happen if Jesus walked into the typical meeting of the typical women's organization of the typical church with its typical decorations of tea bags and sandwiches, and brought with him a woman and seating her among them, said: "Ladies, I found this prostitute out on the street soliciting. Won't you give her a cup of tea?" I don't pretend to know what would happen; maybe she'd get her tea. I hope so. But I imagine that by the time funeral services had been held for heart failures caused by Jesus' introduction, there wouldn't be much left of that women's organization or maybe even of the church which sponsored it.

Perhaps, my speaking from a pulpit about Jesus doing this kind of thing does itself seem a breach of good taste. If it does, I offer my apology, not to Jesus, for I'm sure he wouldn't mind, but to you. Nevertheless, I would like to suggest that good taste which becomes goody-good may itself be the worst of bad taste. Certainly the goody-good taste which refuses to discuss evil, much less deal with it, is in no way hindering the growth of evil and may be encouraging it.

But the cult of goody-good taste which exists in many places — including many churches — is not the worst form in which the art of not dealing with evil is taught. The worst form of this escapist art is practiced by those who think that evil is an illusion. Here the cult of good taste is sanctified in religion in such a degree that not only is it not good taste to see evil or to speak of evil; good taste in this sancti-

fied form means that you must not even think of evil.
It means that just in case you should suffer the "illusion" of an idea of evil you are at once to force your
mind away from any consideration of the evil into
the idea that all is good — and evil is imaginary.
And if you are unable to perform this simple trick
of concentration for yourself then you have at your
command others who will help you.

So far as I can see, Hitler made a major mistake
in starting a war when he did. If he had really wanted
to win the war he should have sent his tourist army
over here for a few years as missionaries for the
idea that evil is illusion. He should have instructed
his henchmen to teach us that all we had to do was
see no evil, hear no evil, speak no evil, and think of
no evil, and then we should all be perfect. His in-
structors would have had much help from people
here, already believing that all was sweetness and
light. And in ten years of high-powered propaganda
and many testimonial meetings he should have convinced us all. After that he could kill us all at leisure.
Since we would then be blind to evil, deaf to evil,
unable even to think of evil, he could have moved
amongst us, unseen, unheard, and unthought of. He
could have done his worst with us. The worst we
could have done to him would be to suppose him an
"illusion" to be thought, or read, out of the country.

Perhaps you think I am too hard on this attempt
of people to escape evil by thinking it an illusion.
I do not mean to be. I only mean to say that it seems
to me that the surest way to let evil forces triumph
in the world is to refuse to think that they exist.

The Nazis almost beat us because for years people

refused to believe that the Nazis were real. "It wasn't possible," we said! Maybe they weren't "possible" to our blind, deaf, unthinking minds which in supreme goody-good taste refused all idea of them. But they were and they are real. And one reason they are real today and still powerful is precisely because we refused to recognize them then.

The idea and the philosophy which declares that evil is an illusion is itself an evil delusion. And the sooner we recover our sanity and face and fight evil for what it is, the sooner we will get better as persons and as society. Perhaps I feel so strongly about the theory that evil is illusion not only because I think it an escapist form of ethical nihilism but also because in my emotional life I felt its potential curse at a very early age.

When I was twelve my best friend, a lad of my own age, was taken ill. His parents thought all evil an illusion including the evil of disease. So it was that when he first complained of headache and soreness they assured him he was perfectly well. The following day he didn't feel like playing the piano at which he was a genius. I still thrill with the sense of his nimble fingers bounding over the keys. When after school that day he went up to bed instead of playing the piano, his mother was frightened. She sat beside him on the bed and read reassuring words to him. Later she called on others to come in to read to him. She had several people employed in town to think and pray and read. But slowly through the hours my young friend's head was pulled back on the pillow as if by a steel cable and held there tight. Fear came at last: good healthy fear of a real evil came at last to both parents, fear for their son's life. I was in the house when they called the doctor. I was there when he arrived. I was there when he came down stairs after seeing my young friend. I can't imagine Jesus seeming any more righteous in his wrath at the money-changers, than did that doctor as he ranted out his anger. "Why call me now — when he will probably die? Why call me to save him for a life as a cripple? Why . . .?" But the doctor's judgment regarding my friend was too much for me. I stole from the room amidst his continuing tirade. I didn't understand then what it all meant. Later I did understand. My friend had what was called spinal meningitis. If the doctor had been called earlier perhaps my friend might not have been a cripple for life, his hands and legs drawn tight upon themselves, unable any more to play a piano. I have sat long hours with that friend since the doctor's tirade. I have sat before a phonograph for hours with him and watched the ecstasy come and go in his eyes as he detected the talent of a fine pianist behind the sounding orchestra. His own, once nimble, fingers are now paralyzed with evil disease. I have sat with him and learned, not in my head, but in my heart, the evil that can come from not believing in the reality of evil.

The delusion of not believing in the reality of evil may be pleasant to thousands — while the delusion lasts. But to other thousands, for whom it has failed the acid test in a trial with real evil, the pleasant faith has turned into a curse. The art of not dealing with evil is discovered at last a sham and a fraud. It is a dangerous sham, a vile fraud! So I say we need the pessimists, all of them, to balance the blind and bleating optimists in this world, who see, hear, and think, of no evil at all. We need people to cry out against all evils. Goody-good taste should not stop them. Goody-good taste sanctified into a religion should not stop other religious people from facing squarely the evils of this life and dealing with them to make a better world.

Ideally, of course, most people are not either hopeless pessimists or deluded optimists. Ideally all of us should be what those parents in the Christmas story tried to make their two boys, one of whom was rapidly becoming an incurable pessimist, the other a Pollyanna optimist. The parents at Christmas time decided to try to balance their youngsters' personality. They bought a pony, and on Christmas eve in the stocking of the pessimist they put a note which read: "In the barn you will find your Shetland pony. Merry Christmas!" And in the stocking of the optimist they placed some dried horse dung and nothing else. Came Christmas morning and the little pessimist reached into his stocking, found and read his note, turned to his parents and said: "If you think you are going to get me to go to the barn just to make a fool of me, you are mistaken. Pony! That's an old gag!" But the optimist when he reached in his sock took a quick look in his hand, looked again more carefully, then shouted joyously: "Mother! Father! I got a pony, too — but he got away!"

Well, there is such a thing as a balanced personality, and all of us ought to try to be one. Not blind optimism which sees no evil and believes in no evil! Not hopeless pessimism which sees no possible good. Instead, we need all of us to stand fearless in the midst of reality, facing the evils as they exist, and working strenuously, help into being the better day that may be our birthright.

VI

THE WORST ENEMY
OF THE BETTER

EVERYBODY HAS SOME kind of an ideal. By which, of
course, I am not suggesting that anybody's ideal is
exactly like anyone else's. In this regard ideals are
very much like consciences which they motivate.
Everybody has a conscience which, though sometimes quite still and often quite small, is nevertheless
a voice sufficient to be heard. So everyone is moti-
vated by some kind of an ideal. It may be an ideal
held only for one's self. More people than most of
us realize in these days care only about themselves.
But butchers, bakers, merchants, thieves, be they
ever so wrapped up in themselves, have an ideal at
least of what they themselves should want and should
have from life and maybe from afterlife.

Of course, most of us have far more than a merely
egocentric ideal. Most of us have ideals of or for
our husbands, our wives, our children and our friends.
We may even go so far as to have ideals of, or for,
other people's children. Indeed, I suspect that most
of us go even further. We have ideals for our
community; for our political party; for the State Department; for Labor; for Capital; for the government of the United States; for the government of
Great Britain; for the government of China; for the
government of the Soviet Union; for the government
of Argentina; for the government of Spain, etc., etc.,

including and culminating in our ideal for a United Nations and a World Government.

An ideal is an imagined better. It is possible to think of an ideal motorcar, an ideal fishing rod, or an ideal king. I have even heard State Department officials speak of the advisability of a benevolent dictatorship for South American countries, from which I gather that in some minds there are even ideals of dictatorship. And, of course, one must not overlook the fact that there can exist the ideal of not having ideals. Some people really try it.

Philosopher Plato, at the opposite extreme, built a world in his imagination which consisted of his ideals of everything! In Plato's perfect world of ideas, where the ideal of everything existed, we may well imagine perfect "men" and perfect "women" making perfect "love" in the park called Perfection, while the perfect "trees" whispered perfect "nothings" to one another in accompaniment of perfect bird "songs" while beneath the tree a perfect set of "beefsteaks" named Ferdinand munched at the perfect "grass" in perfect "content" as he mooed among the perfect "flowers." Indeed, Plato, and not a few philosophers since his time, have suggested that our world with its imperfect men and women and trees and birds and beef animals and flowers depends for its imperfect reality on the "higher" and perfectly ideal "reality" of his "pre-existent world" of ideal ideas.

The Christian religion in most of its early branches followed in Plato's thinking to develop the ideal, the perfect life which it called heaven. And since that time sundry sociological philosophers have tried to

bring heavenly ideals to earth in imaginative idealism
of a type which one of them, Sir Thomas More, in
1516, labeled *Utopia*. Sir Thomas incidentally made
up his label from two Greek words which taken together mean literally: nowhere. Now, you may, if
you like, imagine this sermon merely an extension
of a debate between Plato, who claimed the world of
perfect ideas was the real world, and Sir Thomas
More, who projected in a book an ideal society but
suggested that it had little reality by calling the book
Utopia — or nowhere.

However, I am fairly sure that most of you have
already made up your minds on the matter of the
reality or the unreality of ideal worlds. I feel quite
certain that most of you don't believe in the actual
existence of Plato's perfect world of perfect ideals.
There is no reason, therefore, why I should carry on
an ancient debate when you, the judges, have your
minds made up on one side. Plato has lost the debate!
The perfect world does not exist. Indeed, it may
never exist. Perfect "people," "cows," or "trees" are
out of the question in the real world you know. We
don't believe in the reality of high and mighty ideals
soaring individually or in organization to perfection.
We are liberals, practical people, striving only for
the better. We are finite human beings, humble and
seeking. We are realists. No high-flown ideals of
perfection for us! Not in this life nor in any other!
We are liberals in ethical religion.

I have heard us talk that way. Indeed, I am sure
that most of us think we think that way. Our ideal
is to have practical ideals, achievable ideals, dynamic
ideals, working ideals — ideals as goals. We don't

care for Utopian ideals! We despise perfect ideals! The best is too far away for our practicality. We have enough work to do if only we strive to realize the better. This is our ideal of ourselves. This is the way most of us think and speak.

Yet, despite all our protestations in favor of realistic, creative, practical ideals, I trust I may be pardoned if I suggest that I frequently have more than a suspicion that we are not as free from absolute ideals in practice as we are in our speech. Perhaps we, like a certain famous lady in Shakespeare's *Hamlet*, do in this matter "protest too much" our own innocence.

Let's ask ourselves some questions. Am I an humble person? A practical ideal is a goal to be achieved. It demands work in the direction of the goal. A practical goal is potentially achievable, but since it is not yet achieved, we are humble before it. That is, we distinguish between where we are and where we want to be. In the face of the practical ideal, practically held, our attitude is that of an humble, patient worker. Or am I arrogant? That is, do I arrogate to myself, as if I already possessed them, the qualities of my ideal? Thus the ideal of the scientific method is to discover an objective truth in a limited field of knowledge, on the basis of which more or less accurate predictions may be made. But suppose that I speak "as a scientist" and you and I both feel that when I speak, I speak as if I already had the whole truth and an absolutely certain ability to predict with accuracy. Am I humble then? Do I work at research in science? No I am not. No I do not. I am not humble and I do not work much to find the truth because I have arrogated to myself the virtue of my ideal by Plato's imaginative trick. I am a little like the Pharisee in Jesus' parable who "prayed." And though I say I despise Plato's absolute idealism, I have, without knowing it, my own brands. And naturally I don't work much to enlarge the truth because I have tricked myself into thinking I already have it. The fact that society for two thousand years has been overrun with absolute ideals, and still is, tricks many of us into believing them before most of us ever start to think.

Here is another question: Do I drive myself to the realization of my ideal, or does the ideal drive me? Some of you sometime may have heard somewhere of nagging wives and domineering husbands. Now I am quite sure that the chief reasons that most of us married were two: first, we were driven by a biological urge to mate. Secondly, we were possessed of an ideal of what a mate should be and we thought we had found it. So out of biological need we married an ideal mate. And some of us, I suspect, having married the ideal mate, have never got over the shock of awakening to life some weeks, months or years later, with the real mate. Now, of course, I think that a husband and wife should have practical ideals of what husbands and wives should be. I think they should be humble and at the same time work at their ideals together and alone. But what happens frequently, is that husbands and wives who married ideal mates won't make the mate-ideal practical. Instead in their wifely and husbandly ways they tend to worship the ideal and torment the actual mate.

A domineering husband in love with his ideal wife

naturally does not beat his real wife with clubs—at least not often or much in modern society. No, his beatings are more subtle these days than when the hair on his cave-man chest was thicker. Nowadays a man starts to beat his wife for not being his ideal by telling her she is not what he thought she was. That is generally followed by jokes about how women fool men into marriage; and when such methods as asking her why she doesn't ever cook an interesting meal finally fail, the marriage ends by his remaining in love with his ideal mate even as he at last learns with fairly full heart to hate his real one.

Shades of Plato! Is such a man trying to live with a mate or with an ideal? But what is a woman's "nagging?" Why, it is the persistent worship she pays to the ideal mate she married. "Honey, you forgot to do this." "Sweetie, why can't you remember to do that?" "Hubbie, you know how much I dislike you to —," and "Darling, won't you just this once please me?" Etc., etc., until at last she implores the court to restore to her her maiden name! And if she changes husbands ten times in her lifetime, she will probably always be driven by her ideal-of-a-mate to nag the real one into the divorce courts. She's a victim of the pretty ideal, not of the practical. She's driven by it and she half-way knows it. To her girl friends she may even confess that she knows she shouldn't nag, but "he is so exasperating." And so she does nag.

Two people with practical ideals for one another and shared ideals find marriage and work and families and social responsibilities difficult enough without each of them in addition trying to worship an ideal mate who acts like Rudolph Valentino, or Gloria Swanson. If you are driven to do what you know are foolish, unwise, immoral, selfish things by an ideal you have of mate, children, friends, of an institution, a community, then beware. Beware, for then your ideal of the best man, woman, child, friend, city or state is interfering with your making the situation in which you live even a little better. Beware of compulsive, absolute idealism.

An ideal of the absolutely best may well be the greatest enemy of the better. "The best is the worst enemy of the better." That is an old French proverb and it should have deep meaning and significance for liberals in religion. Indeed, I think it has a special kind of cogency in a liberal church. Most of you who are members of this church are so because you believe that this church is superior to many other churches. And that goal I trust you will help to realize. You do not expect to hear the old, obsolete idealism preached in the pulpit. You do not expect to be asked to believe in the old superstitions of supernaturalism in this church. You do not expect to meet prissy minds, goody-goodiness, vacuous groups, dictatorial power drives, fascist propaganda in this church. For these are some of the things you detest about some other churches you have known. And in your detestation you are, I think, right. We have a different and, I hope, a better ideal in this church.

But shall we arrogate to ourselves the higher virtues to which we aspire as liberals without in humility striving for their fulfillment? This is a human institution. That statement standing by itself should make us humble. There may be ways in which this church will sometimes be worse than other churches. After all, we have no direct or exclusive claim to universal truth or God's righteousness which other churches talk about a good deal. What but our self-disciplined sense of common humanity; what but our humility in search and persistent effort; what but our free discussion seeking understanding; what but ourselves and other human beings seeking and searching for a better do we have to make us better? If we are a better church than most churches it will be because we, who are the church, are striving in humility and persistence for that better. But imagine for a moment that we are suddenly what we aspire to be! Then we become as bad as any.

Really, you don't even have to believe that you possess the best to be menaced by it in personal and institutional life. An ideal to be practical must be related to the possibilities that exist for its realization in some foreseeable future. An ideal which has no possibility of realization in time is a dream and a dangerous dream at that. And while pleasant dreaming is pleasant, it is just as important to know you are dreaming when the dream is good as it is satisfying to wake up from a bad dream to discover that it was "only a dream." It is very easy in our society with its authoritarian dreams of world power, world conquest, world enslavement, world monopoly, world war, to be a victim of Gargantuan ideals. This is as true for individuals, whose civic teachers told them that in a democracy anybody could be president, as it is for churches with illusions of perfection, or cities which are "made of magic," or nations which are "the best in the world."

Absolute idealism — high and mighty idealism — approaches very close to insanity. How sane is the poor, dumb wage-earner who takes food from the mouths of his children in order to burn a candle before a shrine, the burning of which is presumed to have the power to turn the head of the universe in his favor. How sane is the average bobby-soxer who imagines that Frank Sinatra is singing on a phonograph record "only for her." How sane would a man or a woman be who came into any democratic organization which had at least a dozen active people in it believing that he or she could run that group precisely as he or she desired? To have a word in it, to share in discussion, to help in the good work, to be a force among other forces, that, of course, any man or woman could and should be in any democratic society. But to run it as you wish, that is a dictator's dream. To make it come true, people must first be drugged asleep; then their feeble wills must be divided by friction and tensions and fear of violence must threaten.

Many of them prove themselves not at all sane. When they fail to realize their perfect ideal of themselves in that group they go off in a pout. "Play the way I want — or I won't play." Childishness, of course. "Work the way I want to work or I won't work." What is that? How sane are any of us who adopt the ideal of perfect health for ourselves on the presumption that it will last forever? Perfectionism in anything is fraught with danger.

One moment people love an institution, work for

it, give to it. It is an ideal of their life. But let a
new officer be elected, let an old member make an
unpopular suggestion, let somebody's suggestion or
plan be approved instead of their own and suddenly
it isn't exactly pleasant practice which results. When
high ego-ideals are thwarted and frustrated by life,
by reality, then there is danger, danger to individual
sanity, danger to institutional well-being. Beware the
frustrated idealist in yourself. Beware the ideal
which towers into the dreamy heights of perfectionism. Beware your personal dreams of power and perfection. The perfect ideal is frequently the worst
enemy of the real accomplishment of the better. A
frustrated idealist is frequently a saboteur of anything better. Don't hold on to your insanely high
ideals and end up hating yourself because you cannot
accomplish them. Adjust your ideals to possible
achievement. Don't cling to ideals of perfection
which are unattainable by your mate, children,
friends, institutions or yourself; don't cling to the
ideals and come to detest the mate, child, friends, institution and yourself so much so that you must invent
gross or subtle ways to torment, to nag, to sabotage,
to wreck, to terrorize that mate, child, friend, institution. I say to myself; I say it to your neighbors
and I say it to you: the best may be the worst enemy
of the better! Beware the high and holy, the perfect
ideal. Develop in your lives practical ideals for
which you can in humility and patience work to make
yourself and all of life significantly better. Beware
of perfection! Seek the better! The better — if you
really work at it — is good enough for ordinary hu-

mans. I will be content with that; and so, I expect,
will be the laughing stars in the serenity of purple
night. As Marcus Aurelius said,

> "Men exist for one another.
> Teach them then — or
> bear with them."

VII

THE DANGERS OF
BEING INTELLIGENT

BUDDHISM HAS BEEN CALLED the religion of con-
templation. Mohammedanism is known as the religion of action. Christianity is referred to as the
religion of love. The Unitarian religion, too, through
the centuries of its growth, has received its particular designation. Unitarianism has been often called
the religion of intelligence. Were you to walk into a
Unitarian church in Adelaide, Australia; in Prague,
Czechoslovakia; in Birmingham, England; in Delhi,
India; in San Francisco or Boston or Miami, U.S.A.,
you would probably find some of the most intelligent
people of the community gathered together for the
purposes of mental stimulation and proud to be
known as members of "a reasonable faith."

Far be it from me to decry the use of intelligence
in religion or anywhere else. There is not nearly
enough intelligent faith in this world. Not even Unitarians are as intelligent as they can be and as they
ought to be. Certainly no person or no group of
persons can ever become, really, too intelligent. The
critical attitude, the attitude of careful questioning
and sober judgment, is one of the desperate needs of
humanity generally. More and more deeply do we
need to search into the order of the universe. More
and more sternly do we need to probe and pry into
the inner workings of that universe within us we

call the mind. And more and more widely should these results of intelligent research and judgment be spread to more and more people in the world. As a cure for the pretenses and prejudices of the world, intelligence is needed. To uncover and dethrone self-seeking chicanery and deceit in high places, intelligence is needed. To unmask hate — intelligence is needed. To guide our feet in the uncertain future, intelligence is needed. Give us more and more and more intelligence. Give the world's need, more and more and more critically questing persons.

And then what? Well, the stock answer has it that if everyone in the world was a critically intelligent person we should have our perfect world. But, I am not so sure. I believe in intelligence all right. We do need more intelligence, not less. But I am not sure that intelligence alone will produce Utopia. I am not even sure that a cultivation of critical judgment alone will ever make the world even a little better. Indeed, cultivating intelligence alone can make the world worse. I remember walking out of a mortuary one day after having conducted the funeral of a middle-aged mother. On either side of me as I came out, were two of her three youngsters, both of them of high school age. As we came out to the curb and stood under a canopy waiting for a car to come up for us, two doctors stood near by, friends of the mother whose husband was himself a doctor. They were discussing the deceased woman. "It was a long time," I heard one of them say. "Ten months," replied the other. "I wonder how much weight she lost?" asked the first. "Well, it was at least seventy pounds." This answer brought a low whistle from the other physician, and then he said: "Jesus, that's real dehydration." It was raining and we were all under the canopy together, the doctors with their backs to us looking out into the rain. I tried to cover up the painful silence following their remarks, but the youngest girl had plainly heard them and for reasons which some of you may understand, broke into violent weeping. A year later, recalling that incident still made her shudder. And the doctor who made it couldn't understand, until I told him, why that youngster could never bear, after that, being anywhere near him. Nor did it change her feelings when I told her that the doctor was only using his professionally critical intelligence to extend his knowledge. Her reply to me when I told her that was: "He's a beast!"

To tell you the truth I found it hard to disagree with her, and so we agreed that we would go and talk to her father about it, he being also a doctor. Mind you, this was a year after her mother's death and she was still hurt and bitter as she told her father the story. I expected him to tell her of the medical profession, of its ideals, of its need for facts, of its objectivity. I expected him to tell her that the man who made the observation which had hurt her so, was a crack surgeon, a man high in his profession and much used to looking death in the face. Instead when she was through he got up from his desk, walked over to his daughter, put an arm, clumsy with affection, about her and as he patted her he turned to me and with only slightly bitter compassion said of his professional friend: "George always was a heartless bastard."

"Bob," I said, "George might only have been thoughtless." With firm and added bitterness he repeated "George is heartless!" After a few minutes the doctor sent his daughter away and then he told me stories of George, his friend, and how marvelous he was at operating and how in the sick room afterwards what a menace he was. Strange combination, you may say. But not, I think, nearly as extraordinary as it may seem. You see — critical intelligence like any other personal quality is achieved by practice. You hear, you read, you see something. And critical intelligence asks: what, when, where, how, why? Am I seeing what I think I see? Does he mean what he says? Is that interpretation right? Have you got all the facts? These are important scientific questions. Asking them, seeking for answers to them, is cultivating intelligence.

"A wise man holds himself in check," so the poet says, and as he holds himself so, he formulates the question which, in its answer, may make him wiser still. And holding oneself back, cocking an eye, asking the eternal question can become a habit. "A wise man holds himself in check, the fools and poets run ahead." Yes, the fools and poets run ahead, moved by every plea, victims of every crackpot, easy prey for the eager propagandist. "Thank God for the common man: he is so easy to fool!" So say the propagandists.

Do you want to be a fool? Well, most of us don't and so, to be safe, to be sure, we try to make critical questioning a habit of life. And that, I suggest, can be, and is, dangerous. It is dangerous to try to be too safe. "A wise man shuts his doors at night and pulls the bolts and drops the bars." Yes, the wise man, yes, the critical intelligence does and yet — "One must go trustful through the dark. To earn the friendship of the stars." And that, my friends, is one of the dangers of intelligence: that we miss the stars altogether. We can be so confoundedly and continually critical of everything and everybody that we are able to appreciate nothing at all. George the doctor was so interested in dehydration in bodies that he honestly didn't know, so completely was he victim of the critical habit, the difference between a post-mortem examination and a funeral. He didn't know in his blind intelligence that people have feelings. He didn't act as if he knew! He was a super-critical, super-intelligent, heartless beast.

Certainly, we need more intelligent people in the world, in this community, in this and every church, but if our constant and continual seeking, prying, questioning, becomes an unremitting habit with us and leaves us stony-hearted animals, is the world made perfect thereby?

Answer this question! Is that man ignorant who organized a handful of malcontents and enlarged them in a few short years so that they could take over power in a great nation? Is that paper hanger dumb who so carefully and critically gauged every weakness of his enemies that with a few men he could annex two nations to his own? Is that man not intelligent who prepared a nation for war, beat several other nations on the field of battle, in great part by clever psychology? And is the world a Utopia because Hitlerian intelligence and its results run rampant in the world today? A vile and bloody beast is loosed upon us, a heartless witch with all the marshaled intelligence of all the scientists and critical thinkers at his command. He it is, and what he and others like him stand for and what they plan at home and abroad that threatens civilization. Utopia, out of intelligence? Not out of Hitler's intelligence, certainly not; a beast turned loose instead! If critical intelligence be a person's sole qualification it may qualify him best for a jail-yard job of crushing rocks. Remember the sinister and cunning intelligence of a Hitler or a Himmler, then tell me if intelligence alone can make a man?

No, my friends — to believe that intelligence is everything is in itself dangerous. And to employ one's critical faculties only is to stifle a part — a fine part — of our human nature. Man may be a rational animal, but people are also social beings and to cultivate rationality without cultivating in the same degree a social sense is to become an unbalanced person. You can know all anybody knows if you share that knowledge, if you stay close in the society of other people, if you try to teach others and try to help others; then they will call you friend and you will feel them so. But let yourself start believing that your superior knowledge makes them scum by comparison. Go on building yourself up as wise, and scorning others as ignorant, and others will come to suspect you, will sense your attitude of superiority, will shun you and all your wisdom; then, you couldn't help others even if you wanted to. Then, you can justify yourself only by thinking that others shun you because they do not like the truth (which may possibly be so) and you are apt to try to defend yourself, not the truth, by building up philosophies about superior and inferior beings — with yourself among the superior, of course.

The truth is unpopular enough as it is, and difficult to spread without having those who have some grasp on it hug it to themselves with a self-centered sense of superiority. And if by using intelligence in one moment of your life you have gained knowledge, don't let that knowledge die with you by refusing to cultivate your appreciative social nature, so cutting yourself off from those persons whom you might benefit by sharing what you believe you know.

It is all very well in some moments of life "To look on love with disenamoured eyes; To see, with gaze relentless, rendered clear of hope or hatred, of desire or fear. . . ."[1] We become intelligent that way. But you do yourselves and your friends an injustice if you fail to look or cannot see at other times—in a different way, with sympathetic eyes, what goes on in the heart of your friend's young daughter as she follows her mother's body to its grave.

Yes, we should criticize, and so learn, critically. But by all that is holy and best in us need we do nothing but criticize? Is it impossible to be a rational being and still be an appreciative, loving person? I tell you in the words of Paul's letter to the Corinthians:

> "Though I have the gift of prophecy, and
> understand all mysteries and all knowl-
> edge . . . and have not love, I am noth-
> ing."

[1]Clark Ashton Smith, "Transcendence," *Great Poems of the English Language,* ed. Wallace Alvin Briggs, (New York, 1933), p. 1338.

They wheeled the dead body of a woman out in the rain and a man who had sat at her table, a man who smoked his cigar and went to sleep when she played fine music after dinner, now with his back turned on the event of her body's departure from life, said: "Jesus, that's real dehydration." Had he been more than a critical intelligence, had he been a fearless, sympathetic, appreciative, loving soul as well, he might have said softly under his professional breath, "terrific dehydration." But just as truly in fine and deep feeling he might have gone home and written:

"Music I heard with you was more than music,
And bread I broke with you was more than bread;
Now, that I am without you all is desolate;
All that was once so beautiful is dead."[2]

He might have written it. He didn't, for he was merely an intelligent man and so cursed with being "heartless." His was an analytic mind that prevented his sympathetic self from living.

I think we have hold of a principle here which if rightly used will throw light on a fact which is much mentioned. I have heard it said in many places that Unitarians, those same intelligent Unitarians, cannot sing! Now I think I know why. Unitarians are practiced critics who can raise an eyebrow with the best of them. Unitarians are hard to fool, are apt to have read much and studied some, but they can't, so it is said, sing.

The reason I suspect lies, not in a physical handicap, but rather in a psychological habit. Unitarians

[2]Conrad Aiken, "Bread and Music," *The Standard Book of British and American Verse,* ed. Nella Brady. (Garden City, 1932), p. 731.

as a group are apt to be chronic critics. Those of them who enjoy music want it to be perfect, so their criticism will find no faults. But those who enjoy "the best" music and those to whom music is so much noise, think that entering into the spirit of hymn singing somehow degrades them. How, for instance, can you throw yourself, imperfect voice and all, into the lusty singing of a hymn and still sit back and hear whether it sounds all right as music? How can you give yourselves up to the rapture of heart-free, full-throated, group song and at the same time read the words of the hymn with critical eye to discover if all the prepositions are in the right place and the capital letters not in the wrong place to fit into your particular theology? Faced with these alternative tasks many Unitarians choose their habitual role of critic. They listen to others sing — there are some others, we hope — and they read the words to discover whether the minister's selection fits with their theology. Unitarians don't sing more because they find it difficult to change their habitual critical clothes for the somewhat more shabby but friendlier vesture of appreciation in togetherness.

One of the dangers of critical intelligence is that it will ruin you as a hymn singer. And while we are on the subject of Unitarians and the dangers of intelligence, let us solve another mystery. Sometimes I have felt that Unitarians must indeed be a group of very tired liberals. Sometimes I picture them pulling weary flesh and bones together of a Sunday morning and dragging themselves to church. Sometimes indeed I have wondered if any collapsed on the way.

I have wondered so, because when I see them as

the service begins, it seems that suddenly their energy
fails them and they collapse, reaching a rear seat
just in the nick of time! Seriously now — why do
Unitarians like back seats? Why? I rather suspect
it is because a back seat is psychologically a critical
vantage point, a place from which

> "To look . . . with disenamoured eyes,
> To see with gaze relentless,
> Rendered clear of hope or hatred,
> Of desire or fear. . . ."[3]

"Let's listen to this business critically." "Let's
not allow ourselves to be pulled into full participation." "Let's not get emotionally involved in this."
"Let's sit back, let's see. . . . Take a back seat!"
My friends, let's not be afraid to criticize the most
sacred thing. But neither let us be afraid of our
hearts; let us not be afraid to give ourselves emotionally to singing, to participating in worship, to
loving our fellows, to living our lives. Let us be more
than critical analysts. Let us also be appreciative
artists.

But, it is liable to hurt! It's dangerous! Don't
tell me. I already know. Give your heart, give an
emotional understanding to the world's pain, to
profiteering ugliness, to the majesty of stars, to the
horror of war, to the terrible, breathless hope of
permanent peace. Give yourself in full-souled appreciation to these realities, live in imaginative sympathy with the worst and the best of life. And of
course it will hurt, but in the joyous hurt of loving
you can learn, if you have the courage, of the flesh

---

[3]Clark Ashton Smith, *op. cit., loc. cit.*

and blood of life which gives the dry bones of criticism their deeper meaning.

For, it isn't only ugliness, that hurts. Beauty too:

"Loveliness has such a way with me,
That I am close to tears, when petals fall
And needs must hide my face behind a wall,
When autumn trees turn red with ecstasy."[4]

Of course it hurts to live if your heart is in the living. What did you think living was? The emasculated self-love which prides itself in the cold security of knowing critically more and more about the skeletal structure of less and less?

We cannot all shut ourselves in the monastic cell or flee the world into the cloistered quiet of a scientific laboratory. We cannot, even if we should. And even the monk and the scientist would be better, fuller persons did they come in courage and in faith along with us as we give ourselves to life.

"One must be credulous or sit
Forever with the living dead."[5]

Choose if you must the dry bones of cold intellectuality. Choose if you must the brittle logic of rationalistic criticism. And I hope you do choose these for one aspect of your lives. But with these alone I cannot find myself content or filled.

To be intelligent is not the whole of living. Living ought also to be love.

Living ought to be both intelligence and love.

In a word: living should be done in wisdom.

[4]Harold Vinal, "Earth Lover," *Great Poems of the English Language,* ed. Wallace Alvin Briggs, (New York, 1933), p. 1335.

[5]Scudder Middleton, "Wisdom," *Great Poems of the English Language,* ed. Wallace Alvin Briggs, (New York, 1933), p. 1326.

VIII

WHY IS MYSTICISM?

ON A CLEAR AUTUMN DAY it is thrilling to walk up
to a fruit-laden apple tree, pull off a ripe red globe
of nectar, dust it off with a coat sleeve or handker-
chief until its shining waxy surface glows with the
attention you give it and then to bite into the juice-
laden fruit. The snap of that first bite, the crackle
beween the teeth, the flow of rich juice around the
tongue, the rich odor in the nostrils, are all part of
that major delight in life which is symbolized in one
word "apple."

The experience of eating an apple is richly varied
and many-faceted. Yet the creative imagination has
a way of pouring all that experience into one moment
and one word in the remembering mind. That is
mysticism. Were I to dwell long on the merits of
apple picking and the virtues of apple eating, it might
not be long before some of you who like to eat apples
would have a sense of apple odor in your nostrils and
the taste of apple juice in your mouth. And if that
happened so that the repeated apple pictures in your
mind led you to feel that you were seeing, smelling
and tasting a real apple, then you would be having
another mystic experience.

Perhaps you have never dwelt in creative sympathy on the great life and tragic death of Jesus of
Nazareth until, like Saint Theresa, you felt an acute
pain in your side like that of the entering sword

which a Roman guard jabbed into the side of the crucified Jesus. But if you had so used your imaginative sympathy and did feel the sense of strong identification with the tortured prophet of Golgotha's cross, then you would have had what is called a mystic experience.

Have you ever felt in all your life, especially during your young life, that God was watching your every act from his heaven in the sky? Have you ever walked in the street with the completely trusting hand of a small youngster in yours and all suddenly felt that you and the youngster were part and parcel of the same life stream? Have you in imagination gazed into the sky on a starlit dark night and felt no vacancy or strangeness between the stars and you? Have you ever been moved to dream of the rich, full, deep physical and spiritual love you yearned for in another body, mind and spirit; and maybe you sometime thereafter found your love and maybe you didn't, but the dream stayed and stays with you? Have you in hungry hours had visions of fried chicken or beefsteak?

If such things have ever happened to you, then you know by experience what I refer to when I use the words "mysticism" and "mystic experience." Most everybody is a little bit of a mystic. One way or another, at one time or another, most of us have practiced mysticism. Mysticism is only a word which we use to refer to our attempts to theorize about the significant reality with which at any particular time we also feel in communion. Love of mate, love of star, love of God, when we feel ourselves one with them, that is a mystical experience. But we are interested in much more than merely describing a variety of religious experience. It is fairly easy to describe the "what" of mysticism. The more interesting question is "why." Why is mysticism?

Traditional Christian mystics claim that union with one of the saints, with the Virgin Mary, with Jesus, or with God, is the highest form of the mystic experience. They explain the "why" of their claimed communion with the heavenly host by declaring that God seeks out the believing heart of man. God, they say, is forever hunting the souls of men and women, wooing their love and communion, striving to win them away from the desires of the flesh and the glories of this world. When a person renounces "the world, the flesh and the devil," then, say the mystics of Christianity, he is free to give his will to God, and communion with God in the mystic experience comes "supernaturally" as a result. As a naturalistic philosopher, I think that there is an alternative answer. As I see it, mysticism is no more complicated a phenomena and no more supernatural than day-dreaming of a meal when you are hungry or of a feeling of the presence of your mate and children when you are away from home.

Mysticism begins in longing, unsatisfied desire, yearning or frustration. The longing is for a release of sexual tensions. The unsatisfied desire is for the secure satisfaction of food and shelter. The yearning is for accomplishment in the direction of an ideal. The frustration which all of us must face is death. Mysticism begins in hunger unsatisfied: sex hunger unsatisfied, food hunger unsatisfied, hunger after the ideal and hunger for life, unsatisfied. The force of a mystic experience begins in a negative fashion with the pressure created by the frustration of natural desires. We are naturally sexual animals. This is precisely what the Christian theologian means when he says that we are born "in sin." We are sexual products, seeking sexually and creatively to reproduce. And the Christian argues that if we will renounce "sinful sexuality" we can enjoy community with God. And he is right! In so far as we can or must renounce, stifle or deny our food or sex hungers or our ambitions for significance or our hopes for a full life, just so far must we consciously or unconsciously seek compensatory satisfactions some other way.

To human imagination the job of compensation is usually assigned. Nor has imagination generally failed us. Look at the youngster of five or seven or nine who has no playmates. He wants society. He wants to develop his ideal of himself as a social creature, but he has no society except adults. So what does his imagination produce out of his frustration? If mama won't have a baby brother for him, he produces his own playmate — imaginary, it is true, but serviceable.

You get hungry as you drive along the highway and behold: a hot dog stand. You stop, eat the hot dog and are on your way thinking of something else. But suppose you are on a life raft five thousand miles from a hot dog stand? You try to catch a fish but can't keep your mind on it for thinking of beefsteaks. Go hungry long enough and certainly you will see and smell and taste and even chew beefsteaks in imagination. You may even see an imaginary island or two to boot! But that kind of a beefsteak won't fill your stomach nor would the mirage island hold you up if you tried to walk on it.

Here, then, in the child without a playmate, and the man without a meal, we see how frustration seeks relief by way of the creative imagination and, though no actual playmate nor actual beefsteak be produced, the force of the frustration is temporarily reduced. The facts are, of course, that most youngsters prefer actual playmates, even unmanageable ones, to mere day dream playmates. But it is equally factual to say that humanity in general, including youngsters, prefers day dream satisfactions to no satisfactions.

Thus, to use Clare Booth Luce's recent description of herself, it is apparently better to feel that you are "the daughter," in spirit, of a Roman Catholic Pope than to feel that you have no father at all, just as I am sure many a middle-aged lady has found that feeling like a "bride of Christ" is better than never feeling like any kind of a bride at all. And just in case you may never have had an imaginary playmate, never dreamed of a beefsteak until your mouth watered, or never felt like a "bride of Christ" and so still don't get the point, may I suggest that, in principle, the social radical may be practicing the same compensatory mysticism when he struggles along in relative poverty being very "happy" in his complete faith that "the revolution" lies certainly just beyond "the next depression."

Mysticism begins with longing, dissatisfaction, yearning and frustration. Whatever the real or imagined object, imaginary playmate or God with which one achieves mystical communion, behind that act, for days or weeks or years, there was a growing force of dissatisfaction.

William James, examining thousands of such mystical unions, observed that all of them began in emotional turmoil, in a period of disquiet, which he called "the dark night of the soul." One more evidence: fourteenth century Germany experienced a great renewal of religious mysticism. Meister Eckhart led that revival in a period when Louis of Bavaria and Frederick of Austria fought a long and devastating war. It was a period more full than most in that day of famines and floods culminating in 1348 in a visitation of the Great Black Plague. Out of such turmoil and suffering, Eckhart founded his "Friends of God" with a resultant new and widespread return to mystical fervor in vast areas of Europe.

If it is true, as I have tried to show, that mysticism begins in personal dissatisfaction, then it should surprise nobody that for three thousand years of western history, mystical religious concepts have flourished and mystical experiences have been common. The world has been full of frustration and human dissatisfaction these last three thousand years. Food and shelter and clothing needs have been difficult to satisfy for most people in most of those years. For at least two thousand of the three thousand years, frustration of the sex instinct has been almost an automatic matter as a result of the "sex is a sin" teaching of the church. The always difficult matter of sexual mating was further complicated by guilt feelings that sex itself, even if you could mate, was evil. And death has always haunted men and women as a reality somehow to be overcome.

What the Christian theologians did to meet the problem of frustration was to accept gross and universal frustration of desire as an inescapable and incurable fact. They couldn't solve the problem of producing physical plenty or of making a sexually satisfactory social life or of making a difficult and frustrated life seem durable and good. So they chose the oriental way of renunciation of desire itself in this life "in order to merit," as they put it, the "rewards" of an "eternal life." They promised that if one gave up sex desires and food desires and success desires and ego desire and life desires, that one would "be rewarded" with a sense of "union with God" even in this life. Yes, it's true. Here is a system that works. It doesn't matter so much that the youngster has no real playmate if he can create one out of his loneliness and his need for companionship and so have *the feeling* of having a playmate. It matters not so much that one has no loving mate in this life if one can pour one's admiration, devotion, loneliness, into the ear of a virgin-pure-and-mild called Mary, or embrace a sacrificial man like Jesus. Your own father may be dead. You can still find a sense of security in "God-the-Father." Yes, that feeling does come to the frustrated faithful. The theory works! *The feeling is produced,* the frustration is significantly lessened. Says Professor J. H. Leube: "God is not known, he is not understood; he is used, sometimes as a meat purveyor, sometimes as moral support, sometimes as friend, sometimes as an object of life,"[1] or as William James says: "So long as men

---

[1] J. H. Leube, "The Contents of Religious Consciousness," *The Monist,* XI (1901), 536.

can use their God, they care very little who he is or even whether he is at all."[2]

But though this system of mystical faith works, whether God and the Virgin Mary "in heaven" are figments of the imagination or are as real as taxes, it is not a system that works consistently or persistently to ease frustration by giving a mystic sense of unity with God. A mystic experience can give one "a sense of the eternal" but unfortunately that sense of eternity always lasts but a fleeting moment. And then — why then, the pressures, the pains and the frustrations of the temporary world are apt to be all the more painfully frustrating.

To "find God" one must forswear the blandishments of the world, the appeal of the flesh and the temptations to conscience; but world and flesh and the ego-ideal are always there to greet us when we return from a voyage of mystic experience. We may on returning hate our bodies, our minds, our desires, our weaknesses, more than ever before and desire purely and permanently to love that other-worldly God. But always, in the morning, hunger assails us anew with the new day and the desire for mating visits us like as not with our evening prayers.

Worse still. Sometimes we may doubt that the father-God exists at all and then we are left torn between faith and doubt. If we successfully beat off the urgency of biological need in us in any moment as an evil, we are defeated the next moment by the returning desire. If we succumb to so-called "temptation" and satisfy a desire in pleasure, the pleasure-

---

[2]William James, *Varieties of Religious Experience*, (New York, 1902), p. 506.

sense is soon turned to guilt feeling at having "sinned." This age-old attempt to kill all desire on this earth as evil, so as to achieve all happiness in another world of perfection, is thus a system which works at best only by fits and starts of mystic union with God interspersed by many dark nights of the struggling soul. Somehow that fitful, mystic union seems rather "artificial." This life may never be a "perfect heaven" on earth but I rather doubt whether it must always be the disjointed torture which it certainly is to those who stand with one foot on the necks of their own strong desires while with the other they strive for sure footing on the battlements of an other-worldly heaven.

Of course we must recognize that experimentation in any new system is dangerous. Hitler, capitalizing on the frustration of modern Germany after the last war, built himself up as a national father, lover and savior and wooed a nation to mystic experience with a power-made "leadership" which ended in war and ruin. He asked women to renounce their rights as persons to follow him and produce sons so as to find their mystic sense of union with the nation. He asked young men to forego thinking and planning for themselves so as to find a mystic joy in the blood-bath of war in which he said Germany would grow. Obviously there is no great improvement in exchanging a faith in a "God-the-Father" with feet of clay for that in a "God-the-Fuehrer" who has a wooden head. If we are not to remain victims of our own compensatory projections of desire, we must take a more radical approach to the reality of our own natures and of nature outside ourselves.

Who said that the world was evil entire and must be renounced? Who said that fleshly desire was automatically a sin to be shunned like a disease? Who said that our ideals of personal significance and a good life on this earth were satanic whisperings? I'll tell you who it was and still is. It was the defeatists who crumble in fear before the first defeat of their desiring. It was a world leadership thousands of years ago which found no chance of satisfying fully the desires of humanity in this world. Today it is those who know there is a chance for all of us to be happy in this world but whose institutional life and identity and importance is threatened should all people become educated, intelligent, freedom-loving, machine-creating, desire-satisfying animals. The old gods would have to lose their lives if a new manhood and a new womanhood were to be allowed to prosper on the earth.

There are today millions of people and their leaders dedicated to the old gods. And they are afraid to desert them because they have no faith in themselves to create even a sporadic happiness in this life. I can understand their fear. I can understand their hatred of any new ideal that threatens their old ideas. And so should you. Yet for all that, it is still our duty to forge ahead in the creation of a new society of minds and bodies, based on the conviction that all hungers of body or soul are real hungers and if in their satisfaction they harm no one on this earth, then God should not be shocked by their satisfaction. We need to strive with renewed faith in ourselves as inventive animals, wary, humble, creative, interested in one another and bent on satisfying our desires for food and shelter and clothing and love and intelligence and self-control and recreation and dignity. We have possibilities for these things of which our fathers two thousand years ago could not even dream. Why not, then, bend our energies to their realization, throw off the old sense of guilt as "sinners" ground into us for hundreds of years, and with free seeking wills and light hearts go about the work of creative life which is our real purpose and our real joy? Of course we shall meet frustration! But in the modern world, let us find our mystical *rapport* and so a way out of dissatisfaction, in the union of our thoughts and hearts and lives with our wives and husbands, our children, our friends, our fellow human beings, our universe.

All mysticism need not be sheer compensatory projection built out of imagination. Love is mysticism and love may have a real object and a creative force and its own life-long rewards, persistent and consistent, as mates and friends may be consistent and persistent.

We are mystical out of frustration, concerning whatever we believe in. The Christian communes with Christ; the Buddhist with Buddha, never the other way round. Myself, I believe myself a part, I feel myself a part, of earth and sky, of wind, sand and stars; I am joined with the destiny of humanity in this universe; I am part of those I imagine in pleasure or pain the world around; I am in intimate communion with those I love. I am a mystic and have mystical experiences every day of my seeing, smelling, hearing, touching, tasting, life. Why am I a mystic? Why, because I have yearnings, unsatisfied desires, longings and frustrations each day of my life, but each day I enjoy at least a little satisfaction of those desires. And that real satisfaction of real desire with real food, real people, real growth in this real world is mystical experience at its best. It is the union of the desiring self with that which is directly and healthily desired. It is communion. It is the joy of living, not in imagination only, but in reality. Dissatisfaction unrelieved may result in mere mysticism. But dissatisfaction may also lead us to create a better world.

IX

WOMEN IN THE
NEW WORLD TO COME

"A WOMAN'S PLACE is in the home!" For almost
three thousand years the history of mankind has been
pointing toward that statement which, strangely
enough, has only in the last hundred years become
really popular. Three thousand three hundred years
ago Aknaton, the Egyptian king, and his queen-wife,
Nofertete, were unaware of the statement, un-
familiar with its implications. A thousand years later,
the sage in the Book of Proverbs was still praising
women for seeking wool and flax; for making garments and rugs; for selling garments to merchants;
for looking over real estate, buying and selling; for
running a household; for opening her mouth with
wisdom; and for sundry other virtues, which made
him, a man, proud to speak of her with his fellows.
But, by the end of the first century B. C., women were
slowly being wooed into the home. The writer of the
First Epistle to Timothy had his conservative influence as he commanded women, "Learn in quietness
with all subjection. Suffer not a woman to teach nor
to usurp authority over the man, but to be in silence."
Women, be quiet!

It took nearly two thousand years more and a
great deal of pressure to get men, and women, too, to
accept the idea not only that women were to be
quiet, but that they were to do even their "being

quiet" at home. But the thing was at last done and in the latter part of the last century men and women, too, did quite broadly agree that a woman's quiet place was in the sometimes unquiet house.

Many is the time I have heard it said in deep assurance that since women were persons (or ought to be persons) of quietly unassuming virtue, there were only two places where their virtue was safe — in church on Sundays, and through the week in their own houses. A woman's place is in the home! I doubt if there is anyone here who is untouched by that designation of the feminine role. And whatever you may think about it, most men and women in the western world will agree that home is the place for women.

I wonder — has it ever occurred to you to try to relate in principle all those groups and peoples who seem to be a special problem? Just after the last war Germany and her allies became special problems. After the last war Russia became a great and flaming problem. For citizens of the United States, particularly in the south, the Negro is a special and weighty problem, and perennially a problem in the Christian world, is the Jew. Then recently, women became more than usually a vexing problem. Now the problem in each of these cases usually consists of trying to find an answer to a single question. The question is — "What shall we do with—?" What shall we do with the Germans, the Communists, the Negro, the Jew, the women—and now the Japanese? The answers we popularly give are usually rather uniform in principle. What shall we do with the Germans? Why, disarm them, or dismember the German nation. What shall we do with the Communists?

Why, send them back to Russia where they all belong. What shall we do with the Negro? Segregate him, of course. And the Jews? Put them in ghettos, naturally. And women? What shall we do with them? Women? Oh, yes, the women, why, a woman's place is in the home!

Do you see the principle? A certain group threatens "our" power, "our" dominance, "our" peace of mind, "our" way, and so "we" try to remove the threat. "We" try to put them back in their place. Germany threatened the dominance of England, and America, and France. So "we" put her in her place, we hoped, and then went to sleep in our blind self-esteem. Communism threatened the world-wide capitalist control, so "we" tried to isolate Russia, and ourselves from her. The Jew has a different faith, a different culture, so "we" try to isolate him. The Negro has a different color skin from ours, so "we" try to use that color to keep him from competing with us. And women? Why, women are not men, and men are the people of affairs who don't want their monopoly of power threatened, so "we" — we males — try to isolate women at home. "We" allies say Germany's place is a place of weakness. Let us keep her there. "We" capitalists say Communism shouldn't spread beyond Russia. Let's keep it there. "We" whites say Negroes shouldn't compete with us. Let us keep them in their easily segregated place. "We" of a Christian culture say the Jews do not belong. Let's keep them out of our sight in the ghetto. "We" males say: "The world is ours, to have and to run. Let "us" keep it for ourselves and away from our wives. "A woman's place is in the home."

There is the principle, illustrated. "We," the dominant, use some kind of discernible difference as a way of marking those who are not to interfere with "our" dominant position. "We," the presently powerful, take advantage of nationality, or economic doctrine, or skin color, or religion, or sex, as a way of continuing our own selves in power. And that is chiefly why· "we," in power, play up national and racial and religious and sex differences. It is to the advantage of those in power to do so.

These three problems are kindred problems in terms of a principle. The Jew, the Negro and the woman have all been exploited and are all of them now exploited by dominant groups. Putting them in their respective types of ghetto is not enough. It does not answer the fundamentally evil exploiter-exploited relationship. It only continues the critical evil, and continues it in the same old hands with the same old force.

"A woman's place is in the home." Do you know what that statement really is? It is the short cut answer which a male-dominated geared-for-scarcity capitalism gives to the problem of mounting machine production. Two hundred years ago many a man argued with his wife that her place was in the woods with an axe, or in the fields with a hay fork, or in the henhouse with an apron on, into which she could gather the eggs. (Incidentally, tending the chickens is usually considered by the farmer to be women's work. The chief reason for this is, of course, that eggs have a messy way of collapsing in male pants' pockets, but usually ride nimbly to the house perfectly intact in a kitchen apron!) Well, anyway, in all re-

corded history, while women have periodically been
under various kinds of subjection, for the most part
the ordinary woman like the ordinary man considered
herself and was considered by others as being a help-
mate on a marital adventure. She may have been a
drudge, so was the man; she may have worked from
dawn till bedtime — so did the man; she may have
labored in the whole family field of interest as far as
her legs or some animals would take her — so did
the man. And she planted, reaped, made cloth,
sewed, bought, sold, butchered and fought, alongside
her husband. Who had the better of it no one asked,
no one cared, for the family unit was the economic,
the educational, the cultural center of life; and it was
the family — husband, wife, children — against the
world. As late as our own colonial period a woman's
place was beside a man; a husband's place was beside
his wife. And if it was not always literally so, in
ploughing or lumbering, or cooking, or raising the
children, this figuratively was certainly true. Men
and women worked it out together, and their special
talents indicated their special work.

But the machine changed that stable family picture,
and is changing it and will change it much more in
the near future than it has already been changed.
The family moved to town — a great part of it did.
And the male member of that family, after being in
the town a generation or two, is the fellow who invented the slogan — " a woman's place is in the
home." He invented it because he was frightened at
what city life and city evils might do to his private
sex-object — wife.

The slogan was invented at first to keep women

from gadding about, getting into mischief in their new city-found spare time. It was advanced when jobs were scarce to send women workers back to their houses. And it came to be accepted as the male club to keep women, who by this time were having smaller families and less housework, from trying a hand at any serious competitive occupation outside the house. The ideal city woman of fifty years ago was one who was all wrapped up in caring for the family, the inside of the house, her French lessons, her sewing and her music. Since that time the movies and radio have robbed her of music making. The United Textile Workers and other garment manufacturers' unions have usurped her sewing job (except needlepoint chair bottoms). French is no longer popular since Petain and Laval were in power. The children are fewer and fewer per family — and father may be a traveling salesman, or an airplane-riding executive, home only on week ends. That leaves a conventional woman, or did, until the war-created manpower shortage, with just the inside of the house for her own. The inside of the house itself had shrunk from a spacious old eight or ten rooms to a modern five- or six-, and frequently to a two-room efficiency apartment, which, if it had bars on the windows, would not be as roomy as an up-to-date jail! And that, my friends, is where women belong! In a home whose functions once included manufacturing and processing, growing and distributing, education and all charity, but which has now shrunk to three rooms and a bedside radio. In this setup, how a woman can keep from becoming neurotic after listening to radio ads between soap serials for just three days, is more than I can fathom. Women must be less suggestible than men!

Still, the radio furnished apartment is a symbol for what is left of the home after the machine age and birth control is through with it. And a woman's place is in a home shrunken from a rich community of interests and labors from a ten-room house with five children to a childless two-room efficiency apartment. A woman's place is in that home, and home isn't even a house. You take it, ladies, I'll take the jail; even the ghetto is roomier imprisonment.

Oh, I know it isn't quite as bad as that for all women, not yet. But if we try to take the slogan seriously, it will be more and more like that for more and more women.

Clearly, however, it ought to be realized that there is enough truth in the symbolic picture I have painted to make all of us know that those who say woman's place is in the home, both men and women, are trying to shout a problem down, rather than deal with it intelligently. Let me speak plainly some convictions. The one major difference between men and women upon which scientists are agreed is that for a short period in the lives of most women they are unable completely to fulfill a normal human role. During the months of pregnancy and immediately thereafter for a few weeks the healthiest woman is unable to compete with other persons, male and female, on an equal footing. But, aside from that single fact of difference there are no innate differences between men and women. There are no innate inferiorities in one sex as a class. There are no inborn and absolutely rigid superiorities in either sex considered as a whole. Mind you, I am not saying that men and women are now biological, or psychological, or economic, or social, equals. We are not equals! Males are, in fact, generally superior physically, and psychologically, and economically, and socially. What is true of present actual male superiority over females is just as true in that realm as is the real superiority of whites over Negroes. And the reasons behind white superiority are almost identical in principle to the reasons for male dominance over women. But it is not innate differences which make the difference! The discrepancy in ability and power between men and women is not innate, is not inborn, even though generally real. The differences are cultivated! They are differences of convention, solidified in tradition, and sanctified in law and culture through the generations. It is certainly true that women do not as a rule get equal pay for equal work. They are as a fact economically inferior in position. Yet it is not impossible for women to produce as much as men, that is, to be really equal in work, and it is not impossible to suppose that women would be able to accept and to spend a pay check equal to that of an equally productive male worker.

The impossibility lies (and with it, the "inferiority") in a tradition of economics. In a changed economic philosophy, in communistic Russia, and increasingly in transmission belt production in this country, equal pay to women in exchange for equal work becomes an accepted axiom in practice. Plainly, the economic philosophy is at fault, not the women. Women would be as good as men in every way except for the time of childbearing if they were given and would take opportunity for development equally with men. And that fact goes far to explain why it is that, in a traditionally male dominated society, women so grudgingly are given equal opportunity.

As it is, it is high time that men realized the suppressive power they wield on feminine personality. Most men are so unconscious of the exploitive traditions in which they were raised that they would be sincerely surprised to learn how suppressive of human talent they really are in blind practice of tradition. One of the most sacred cows of a sacrosanct convention is the one which runs in pious male hearts: "Give the little woman everything!" I have known men who actually worried themselves into nervous wrecks because in their own eyes they failed to live up to that dictum. In practice, what has that prodding, "Give the wife everything," actually done? It has caused many a man to have a nervous breakdown with a tragically unnecessary feeling of inferiority when he fails to live up to it. And if the man succeeds in standing up to the admonition, his wife becomes, unless she be very wise, an exteriorly pretty but spiritually vicious and vacuous parasite. Between the male nervous wrecks and the female parasites produced in an attempt to satisfy a stifling tradition it is time we started thinking in personal terms, rather than in the merely traditional. We have too long — we are now — bowed down to too many sacred cows of tradition. Men, and women no less, are people who ought to enjoy the rights of persons and share together the duties of persons who live in a common society.

In the days to come you are going to hear much

talk about women going back into the home (all three rooms of it) so that returning Army and Navy men can have a job. Back to the jail, ladies! And that is what it means, whether you like to go back or whether you hate it. Conventional economics is the jailer. We wouldn't think of prostituting the lives of millions of women by asking them to give their bodies for the sex satisfaction of the returning Army and Navy men. We wouldn't approve it. Horrors! But we shall, millions of us will, approve sending women, "all women," back to the home even if many have no real home. And we will in that sanction be approving a prostitution of talent and of spirit no less vicious, no less brutal, no less evil in its results than would be the prostitution of body. Back to vacuity — three rooms with the radio always and a movie every other day! Give the little woman everything! Oh, yes, everything, except a meaningful, productive life of labor. We men want that. Sacrifice the women to the system, give the men what they need — a job. Put the little woman on a dusty pedestal.

This kind of thinking you will discern in the new world to come. There will be much of it. And what will you say about it? What will you do about it, you thoughtful men and women? I know what I believe I ought to think and do. Men and women are persons — both need meaningful work. Not men alone, but women, too, need meaningful labor. Men returning from armed services need it. Civilian workers need it. Women need it. If we have to disregard a convention, if we must blow a tradition sky-high, if we ought to change a system that persons in their fundamental need may be served, then let us do it — willfully, quickly. Systems were made to serve persons, not persons to be slaves of a system.

Of this I am sure, that in the new world to come, for many years of it, women and men are going to be less secure, less stable in old traditions and ancient conventions. Change will be heaped upon us even against our wills. The old agrarian family pattern of home life is breaking up. Let that pattern go! It served its time. Let us not cling to it too desperately.

A new pattern of family life is in the borning. A new home is evolving, a spiritual home as spiritually real as is the love I hold for my mother a thousand miles away, yet not dependent on four walls or a frying pan to make it binding. The home of tomorrow will have a physical center in a room or rooms somewhere, among houses on a street or in a high apartment, but that will be only a physical center and we will recognize the fact. Home will be the spiritual reality of trust shared by a mother, father, children, a set of common ideals commonly sought for, discussed and through common family labor achieved. The new home will not be limited geographically by a house or a hedge or a fence. The world will be our new home in the days to come. Increasingly it will be so, and increasingly we shall know it. And in that world men and women shall labor freely, equally, sharing in each other's joys, being consolers of each other's sorrows, loving one another, and their children, in all the chances and changes of their lives. Women will be educated equally with men. Their talents will be used equally with those of men. They will be paid no less than men. Women, no less than men, will be at home in the world and will work in it. That world will be their home.

Yes, in that new world to come, even a man's place will be in the home!

X

MR. CAPITAL AND MRS. LABOR

"CAPITAL" AND "LABOR" are words. Until we know to what we are referring when we use them, they are mere words. Who is a capitalist? Who is a laborer? Some people I know seem to have the feeling that a capitalist is a person who neither worries nor works, while a laborer is a person who works, has no money and many worries. Actually, however, a person can work longer hours, have more worries and at the end of the year have less money than a laborer and still feel himself to be known by others to be a capitalist.

A window decorator in a chain store frequently works twice the hours of a salesgirl in the same store, and when he is through buying the company's stock in weekly installments he has less money to spend than she does. Yet, he feels like a capitalist all the while. His most real pay comes in the odd moments when he dreams of himself as "district-manager-at-$10,000-a-year," a job which he may or may not some day possess. On the other hand a person who owns a house, an automobile and earns ten or twenty-five thousand dollars per year salary may yet be very much against capitalists, and feel himself to be a laborer. Thus possession of money, stocks and bonds does not automatically prevent a person from feeling like a laborer; and a man can be broke and work eighteen hours a day and still feel himself to be a capitalist. As far as I can make out, the word "capitalist" refers to all those people who feel themselves in sympathy with the general tradition, aims and purpose of those who own or manage the great enterprises of our time. Thus some of the people who have the least capital might be loudest in their praise of the capitalists. And the word "laborer" I take it refers to all those people who are in sympathy with the tradition, aims and purposes of that group of people who know themselves to be employed by those who own or manage the great productive enterprises of our time and subject to unemployment at the latter's discretion. How much or how little capital you control; how few or how many hours you actually work, does not automatically determine whether you feel yourself to be a capitalist or a laborer. If you feel sympathy with employing power and aims and values then even though you are an employee you are still a capitalist at heart. If your basic sympathy is with the employee even though you yourself do the hiring and firing, then you are pro-labor. A capitalist is a man who feels like one. A person is part of labor who feels himself so.

The aims of capitalist and laborer are almost identical. Do not both desire to keep what they have of privilege, power, preferment and income? Do not both desire to extend if they can their group privilege, power, preferment and income? Their divergence is not in aim — both seek the same ends. Divergence results from two things. First there is the fact that owners and managers have in the past come to possess a great deal more privilege, power, security and income than was enjoyed by the laborers they employed. And as a result of that fact those employees felt discriminated against, "frozen out" of the more polite society of owners and managers.

Thus, because the owner and manager treated fellow owners and managers as a special kind of animal and other employees as "common" laborers, the laborers themselves in due time also came to feel a special kind of commonality in their common labor. Capitalists, when they began to feel and to act like an uncommon breed of men, developed in some of their employees a counter sense of group feeling as "common" or ordinary laborers. Thus clearly, if anybody is responsible for organized labor feeling itself a special group with special interests, it is the capitalist who first made his employees feel that they were entitled only to common pay while he was entitled to frequently uncommon profits. The owner-manager of old is responsible for labor's sense of separateness from his interests now. The capitalist is responsible for labor organization. And if he does not like it now in its results, he should blame not the labor unions but his own forefather capitalists. Here in a quatrain of Sarah Cleghorn you can learn more about the ethical responsibility for present capital-labor disputes than in most of the treatises that have been written. Listen and learn:

> The golf links lie so near the mill
> That almost every day
> The laboring children can look out
> And see the men at play.[1]

Yes, it happened that way for one, two, three, for ten generations in Europe and America, the ex-

---

[1] *A New Anthology of Modern Poetry,* edited by Selden Rodwen (New York, 1938), p. 148.

ploitive, machine-making, free-enterprising capitalist took bread and meat and gravy and golf courses for himself, gave himself the housing and his children the education and generally was smart enough to put concealing fences about most of his habits and his luxuries. He left his "common labor" employees only uncertain crumbs! Only slowly did the hungry eyes of the undernourished find cracks in the fence to look through and discover how uncommon men lived. But sometimes from three-storied factory windows, the common working people could see the golf course and the uncommon men at play. Then, envy rose in the hearts of employees when want had not already produced its slow hurt in the soul. And men began to bleed and under beatings and bludgeonings began to die for the sake of organizations of common laborers, who in the mere hope of union began to find a hidden strength.

Oh, Mr. Capital was strong. He was intelligent to exploit. He was daring in invention and discovery. He was ruthless in competition and with "his help." And he treated labor even less well than he treated his wife. Mr. Capital roamed the world, but his wife's place was in the home. Mrs. Labor had but to obey. Mr. Capital took the profit and what he chose and sometimes, only if he chose, he shared with Mrs. Labor. And, of course, Mr. Capital paid the priests and the preachers their meager wages to keep sharp eyes on Mrs. Labor, and he didn't have to tell them on which side their bread was buttered. When the churchmen had butter, Mr. Capital bought it for them. — Obviously he was a fine fellow. "Don't criticize Mr. Capital!" So the bought churches,

some of which did and some of which didn't know
they were bought, assured Mr. Capital that he was
God's special gift to man. And as for Mrs. Labor
— well, didn't the Bible say "the poor we have always
with us"?

So did, so still does, most of the church pile its own
sin on the sin of greedy, shortsighted exploitive
men, to draw the line sharp and clear between the
world, the rights and the duties of Mr. Capital and
Mrs. Labor.

So far, I have tried to suggest what the words
capital and labor refer to. They refer, I think, to
the fact that owners and managers of industry first
set themselves apart as uncommon people deserving
of uncommon rewards, as a result of which the common laborer in this world, reacted to organize himself for the sake of discovering something like equal
power to cope with the power of capital.

The capitalist organized himself along class lines
into a specially privileged group in our world. With
that loose-knit organization, he has succeeded in con-
vincing church and state that he had a special right
to his special privileges and so generally in the past
and generally now, both church and state sanction
his still unequal privilege as his right.

I began my ministry at a time when organized labor
was beginning to feel its first organizational strength
on something like a national scale. In those days I
argued and preached for the right of labor to organize and to bargain collectively. I was called
pro-labor and labelled by many as a "Communist"
for so arguing. Basically I was interested in simple
social justice for labor and capital. Why should Mr.

Capital have so much of power and profit and Mrs.
Labor have so little? I argued then and I argue now
that Mr. Capital and Mrs. Labor ought to live together as happy man and wife enjoying the same
rights and privileges and powers. But Mr. Capital,
who got his special interests organized first, doesn't
like that idea of justice. His "unions," probably the
wealthiest and most powerful on earth, organizations
like the National Association of Manufacturers,
seem to think that justice means keeping all you have
and getting more if you can, even if what you already
have is much more proportionately than anybody
else has. Thus, the National Association of Manufacturers' lawyers braintrusted the killing of the
OPA "to bring prices down" and "house building
and production up"[2] — they said. But prices went up,
"31% higher than at OPA's end," and according to
several statements of President Truman, house building has dropped off greatly. While production in
some other things did really rise, the spectacular
change that the OPA's death brought about was a
profit rise which was reported in the *Wall Street
Journal,* amounted to 34%. (Note the source —
Wall Street Journal.)[3] According to its survey, iron
and steel company profits rose 53.7%, rubber goods
company profits rose 103.9%. Textile goods company profits rose 219.9%.

Profits were so high on the basis of new high prices
that David Lawrence, anti-labor columnist, felt
forced in the *United States News* he edits, to write:
"Profits at present levels are turning out to be a

2 Ben Criswell, Herald Business Analyst from U. S. Bureau of
Labor Statistics, *Miami Herald* (September 2, 1947).
3 End of first quarter (1947) reports, April, 1947.

source of embarrassment to many industries. Profit
reports for the first quarter of 1947 will show a rate
of earnings, after taxes, that is well above 1946, a
record year." So, Mr. Lawrence feels that some of
his fellow capitalists will be "embarrassed" by high
profits. Why embarrassed, do you think? Certainly
the OPA was killed precisely to make price rises and
profit-taking higher. But then you know what Mr.
Capital says in the newspapers: "Wages have gone
up, so prices must go up."

The CIO Nathan Report, was, you recall, laughed
and scorned to death in Mr. Capital's newspapers.
Yet, at the moment, with prices high, wages but
grudgingly increased and production up, profits the
first quarter of 1947 are on the average so high as
to be "embarrassing." If profits are embarrassingly
high, the only way Mr. Capital can relieve himself
of his red face is either to raise wages or to cut
prices, both of which were suggested by the Nathan
Report, which only a few months ago was called
many names which a minister is never supposed to
have heard much less repeat in the pulpit.

But though his profits embarrass him as he brings
them bulging home in his pockets for the eyes of Mrs.
Labor to look upon, still Mr. Capital is not content.
He has the pocket-filling angle all worked out, with
the OPA now dead, but he is scared. With food
prices up from 24% to 65%, Mrs. Labor asked for
an increase of from 12½% to 18½% for her
grocery money. Mr. Capital of the bulging 1946
pockets said such an increase would bankrupt him.
But he gave in all along the block, frequently after
the Mrs. Labors on the block had walked out of the

house and insisted on spending days and nights away from home until he increased the grocery money. But, though Mr. Capital gave in, and though his pockets were embarrassingly full at the moment, he was not content. When the wives of the block got to talking, they came back high-hat, acting almost as if they were as good as their husbands. So the Mr. Capitals got together again, and once more visited and beseeched, threatened and cajoled, their dear old Uncle Sam to put out an edict which would keep the wives on the block, once and for all, "in their places." The Mr. Capitals were scared of all the side-walk-marching solidarity and the across-the-back-fence-engendered ideas which the Mrs. Labors all down the block had discovered in themselves. So some time ago, they got Lawyer Ingles who works for Mr. Capital in Allis-Chalmers, Fruehauf Trailer, J. I. Case and Inland Steel to get together with Uncle Sam's representative Mr. Ralph Waldo Gwinn, and Mr. Capital at Chrysler Motors lent his lawyers, and Mr. Capital's Union, the National Association of Manufacturers loaned a half dozen lawyers, all to present Uncle Sam with the edict they want him to impose on Mrs. Labor in every block in the country.

This edict was called the "Taft-Hartley" bill. Uncle Sam was soon convinced that it would be as good for everybody as Mr. Capital said it was. So it is now illegal for the Mrs. Labors to "conspire" to walk out of their kitchens and refuse to cook for Mr. Capital and his cronies. "Collusion" in such demands should be punished by law, says Mr. Capital. Thus, though the Mr. Capitals have been or-

ganized on a nation-wide basis for at least a generation, they are now using their nationally organized
force to see to it that the Mrs. Labors of the nation
never get their heads together from Miami to Maine
to San Francisco.

Of course Mrs. Labor is interested in a conven-
tionally monogamous marriage with Mr. Capital
when they come together for the work and joy and
the rewards implicit in such agreements. Mrs. Labor
is hopeful that Mr. Capital "really means it." She
wants him to say that he will keep himself "only unto
her." She wants a closed shop home—a monogamous
marriage. But Mr. Capital, from long experience,
has enjoyed his power, freedom and privilege. He
wants to come and go as he will; to hold the power,
as a right, to throw his wife out and get someone
else in if he desires. No closed shop for him! He
wants to be "top dog" and surely. Let capital be
free and let labor be tied. To Uncle Sam, Mr. Capital has yelled for several years past "hands off business!" and in the next breath, "Get tough with
labor!" And when the Taft-Hartley bill passed, Mr.
Capital had his way once more with Uncle Sam.

It is my firm faith that in the long run labor will
be strengthened as a result of the passage and administration of the Taft-Hartley Law. In labor
unions there is strength. American labor has so far
discovered only the merest outlines of that fact and
the new labor legislation will teach labor, more than
ever before, that it must stand and work united.

Mr. Capital made a great initial error in treating
himself as an uncommon man and Mrs. Labor as a
common drudge. But after years of believing that

Mr. Capital "knew best," Mrs. Labor is now awake to the fact that labor too is human and worthy of human rights as well as human work. And, at least until labor enjoys those rights fully with capital, labor strength in labor union will grow despite all obstacles.

Many people are saying, and perhaps rightly saying, that the Taft-Hartley Law is the first long step in the direction of fascism. It could be and it may be so. Yet, I like to consider another possibility. That law may be the foundation stone on which a really united labor movement and the beginnings of an American Labor Party may be built. We are at least as much like Great Britain as we are like pre-Nazi Germany. How can we say, surely, that one step toward Fascism will take us the whole journey down that road? In fifteen years this country's government rather than being Fascist may look much more like Great Britain's labor government today. Fascism can happen here; of course it's possible. But can you be sure that a labor government isn't more probable in the long run? To tell you the truth in the family quarrel, Mr. Capital has chosen to generate with Mrs. Labor, I am not at all sure that Mr. Capital will have the last word. That fight can, of course, become as unprofitable for both as would be the fist fight of two boys for one ice cream cone. I have a feeling that we are learning that lesson now, both capital and labor. But in the long run I have the faith that it will be as fruitful as the democratic method, machine technology and a growing social conscience promise it to be.

Our job in church, in government and in labor union is certainly to try to make it so. One final word

— in this address I have used an analogy. I have likened the relations of capital and labor to those of husband and wife. There are two dangers in using analogies. One, of course, is that an analogy frequently oversimplifies a problem. The second danger in the use of an analogy is that it may clearly illustrate some principles underlying a problem and so tend to create that most dangerous of all conditions, human understanding. I know I have yielded, somewhat, to the first danger. I hope you succumb to the second. Capital and labor are facing their first great crisis in America. Another step toward Fascism? Or a step toward a more equal democracy in work than we have ever had. Which will you work for?

XI

THAT MAN — JOHN L. LEWIS

THAT MAN, John L. Lewis, in his lifetime has shown
the same organizing genius and the same ruthlessness
in dealing with his competitors as was employed by
the great money pirate, J. P. Morgan-the-elder who
caused two depressions, one in 1895, the other in
1907. John L. Lewis has used the same violently
suppressive methods on his opponents as those used
by the great business buccaneer, Andrew Carnegie,
who weathered the bloodily famous Homestead
strike of 1892 and fathered the United States Steel
Company whose radio programs you may now
"freely" enjoy. John L. Lewis has the same power-
mad drive which was so notoriously shown forth in
the life of that famed free enterpriser, E. H. Harriman, who, unsatisfied with running a consolidation of
the Union Pacific and Southern Pacific railroads,
threw the country into a panic by his manipulations
in an abortive attempt to take over the Northern
Pacific also. John L. Lewis, dealing in labor, and
John D. Rockefeller, dealing in oil, both flitted after
delusions of grandeur in the "best" traditions of
American capitalism, though, admittedly, the phil-
anthropies of the latter have outdone even the
dreams of John L. Lewis.

John L. Lewis' disregard for the public interest is
typical of all the men I have so far mentioned. His
thwarting of the general welfare to increase his own

power is identical in principle with that employed by the late dollar freebooter, Andrew Mellon, even if not so devastating in effect as was the unbridled private initiative of that purest pirate of them all — Jay (Black Friday) Gould.

In a word, that man, John L. Lewis, as a person, is a big-time operator in the notorious tradition of individualistic, expansionist, monopolistic capitalism. Like most of the other men I have mentioned, John L. Lewis has made his positive contribution to America. But, like them also, he has been willing for the sake of an increase in power to misuse, not only his enemies, but his friends as well. Rejected by Franklin Roosevelt in his demands for high office in the Democratic administration, John L. Lewis turned on Roosevelt and on the best interests of the miners he should have represented and for these last two major elections has functioned as a Republican. Where he will turn or what he will become if the Republicans fail to give him a cabinet post two years hence, I do not dare predict. That he will continue to try to increase the power which has already corroded his humanity, I have no doubt. For power, I think, has gone somewhat to the head of John L. Lewis. To suppose that he has called strikes in the number he has and at the time he has merely to benefit the living standards and working conditions of miners is to be either politically naïve or uninformed or both.

Three coal strikes ago it was said by many in the inner circles of the Democratic administration that Republican mine owners and Republican labor leaders in coal were in unspoken collusion to stage a strike which both silently agreed not to arbitrate until the Democratic administration was "properly embarrassed." True or not, it is certainly possible in both mine owner and labor leader Lewis psychology. During the last strike, called off by an indicted John L. Lewis, it was common knowledge in the Department of the Interior that the Government, which was profitably operating the soft coal mines for the mine owners, wanted to turn the mines back to their owners before the New Year brought a Republican Congress into Washington. Lewis, it is said, countered this government wish by calling a strike which was to last either beyond that time, or was to get a contract of short duration from the mine owners, which, while certainly benefiting the mine workers, would also make the Democrats a laughing stock before the Republicans and the country.

I cannot assess fully the reasons Lewis had for calling the last coal strike, but that it was called for both political and personal-power reasons, over and beyond a will to benefit miners, few intelligent people in Washington or elsewhere would question. Precisely why and exactly how the whole strike was planned, few people can now know. But personal power and big political stakes were in it you can be sure. And John L. Lewis was throwing his force at his opposition for all it was worth and in considerable disregard of the public good. He was doing it in precisely the tradition of the big business buccaneers whom Lewis has for many years fought and from whom he learned most of the lessons he now uses against them.

As a person, then, that man, John L. Lewis, is a

power-hungry, power-corroded, monopoly-seeking, privately venturing, free enterpriser who uses labor rather than bank stocks or oil or steel to advance himself in his competitive climb to fame. But on the positive side, let it not be forgotten that John L. Lewis has been a hard-working, hard-hitting labor organizer, working generally for what he believed would benefit most of the people in these states — the laborers. Let it not be forgotten that it was his CIO vertical type labor union which gave direction and power to a submerged majority of our people and allowed labor at least a fighting chance to balance itself in power against ownership and management in the domestic conflict which continues amongst us for higher purchasing power, decent standards of work and a share in the direction of the economic life of our country. That man, John L. Lewis, deserves his fame as much as any of the other great, if ruthless, organizers and enterprisers in American life I have mentioned.

Of course, I don't think that most people would agree with that judgment. "What! John D. Rockefeller no more worthy of praise than John L. Lewis — that man!" Or, "the great financier, J. P. Morgan, no more worthy of fame than John L. Lewis!" A large part of the public would, I am sure, protest strongly at the comparison. Morgan and Rockefeller, Andrew Mellon and Jay Gould, Andrew Carnegie and E. H. Harriman are great and dignified names in the people's minds. "John L. Lewis" is a name which stands more for infamy than for greatness. Had you thought why this might be? J. P. Morgan sent this country into two devastating major panics and yet was hailed for his personally profitable manipulations as the "savior of his country in distress." That's what one newspaper called him, in the depth of a depression he caused. But when Lewis' miners strike, he becomes (and I quote a "Committee of 100" speaker) "the mightiest totalitarian." An interesting contrast! And seven people out of eight, interviewed on the street by a local newsman, fairly well agreed that "any sentence imposed on John L. Lewis — life or anything else the Judge can think up" wouldn't be too stern a treatment to mete out to that bushy-browed mine leader. Why the different opinions among our countrymen of very similar men?

In asking this question I am not now interested in that man, John L. Lewis, as a person. We are now seeking to discover his significance as a symbol. In beginning this latter inquiry, I turn first to the sharp but gently probing journal, *The New Yorker*. From the issue of December 7, 1946, I quote from the column of A. J. Liebling: "It is too early, as I write, to present a detailed critique of the way our press has handled the news about the coal miners' latest abstention from work. I sometimes fancy, however, that I detect a shift in the papers' economic line since October, when the meat producers were abstaining from the sale of any meat at ceiling prices. Jack Werkley, a *Herald Tribune* reporter, did, it is true, call the October episode a farmers' strike. And Will Lissner, in the *Times,* wrote accurately, if inconspicuously (page 17) that 'the main reason why farmers are buying and growers are holding cattle is that it appears to be profitable.' But, there was a

note of understanding approval, even, I might say,
of affection, in most of the stories about the cattlemen who were represented as rugged, wholesome,
humorous individual enterprisers, standing with their
gum boots solidly planted in hog slop while they told
the rest of the country to meet their terms. Maybe
it is just my imagination, but the papers seem to be
taking a bleaker view of the coal miners, who are
using exactly the same tactics. The cattlemen held
on to their beasts until they got their price, where-
upon meat appeared in quantity. The miners are
withholding their labor, but the press seems to have
missed the parallel. The *Herald Tribune,* which on
October 14 published a long piece about how decontrolled grain prices would affect the cost of raising hogs, has so far printed no companion piece on
how decontrolled meat and other prices affect the
cost of raising miners."

Now actually, the meat strike was a long strike.
It began with threats against OPA and the administration at least a year before the recent election. Large meat producers and meat processors and
meat distributors led the strike. Sympathetically it
spread. The Republican Party seems to have had a
hand in enlarging it. There was "obviously" an
increasing meat shortage and somehow "OPA was
to blame." Take off the OPA ceiling prices and
meat would fall as manna from heaven upon our
tables below. So it was said, in effect, loudly and
long in most places in the press. And in part, at
least, there was truth. Ceilings were taken off meat
and tons of meat were available for the family table.
Overnight we discovered that this manna-from-

heaven-meat, which didn't exist except in our dreams before price ceilings were removed was a higher-priced product by 25% to 50% than ordinary wartime meat. The reason: there was a strike. It was a producers' and processors' strike. It was a strike won. During the strike you had little meat. After the strike you paid and you still pay 25% to 90% more for your meat. It was a strike against the common good. It was a strike against labor. It was a strike against people. It was a strike against fixed incomes. It was a strike against you! But the newspapers for the most part were sympathetic to that strike. And therefore, not the strikers, but the Government representing you and your interest was made the culprit in newspaper criticism. And you were an exceptional person indeed if you didn't follow the strikers' line as day after day it was dished up for you sympathetically in the press. Read the papers long enough and against your will and against your own interest you will find yourself criticizing OPA. A newspaper campaign like that angled against OPA is almost enough to convince me that the fellow was right who said: "The only way you can be intelligent these days is not to be able to read."

Remember another episode. Five and six years ago President Roosevelt was trying to prepare us for war. But the large corporations would not convert or enlarge their plants unless guaranteed a return of capital investment and cost-plus contracts for manufacture. For nearly two years there was a quiet capital strike against the government — against the New Deal. And the capitalists won. The government and the New Deal lost. But did you read about it in all the newspapers all the time? In a very few you read something — yes. In a few others, in obscure places you might have read something more. But the public generally was rallied to favor cost-plus production against its own best interests.

A general in Washington told me recently that that capital strike lengthened the war with Japan by from six months to one year. And you didn't even know, and few will ever know, who led that strike. The conspirators are as nameless as revolutionary plotters. We know their names: their names are great names in American business and banking. But the front page doesn't call them strikers against the government. The reason: most of the press was in sympathy with the capitalist strikers!

So J. P. Morgan is famous! His is a "great name" in a great American family. And John L. Lewis? Are the newspapers sympathetic to his labor strike? For the most part, in the headlines plainly and generally, no! And John L. Lewis, is, therefore, "that man" and "any sentence a Judge can impose on him — life or anything else" is fine, just fine, to seven out of eight people on the streets of Miami. And that despite the fact that the real interest of seven out of eight people on the streets of Miami lies — if you must choose one — with labor! Newspaper and radio sympathy, or lack of sympathy, makes the difference frequently between fame and infamy!

As a minister, I do not think highly of the morals of that man, John L. Lewis. They are as bad, though not quite so devastatingly evil, as those of the other so-called great men I have mentioned. But John L. Lewis is not pilloried in the press because of his morals! The mine owners for the most

part have identical morals and use identical methods
on the other side of the conflict. But they are not
attacked! Here is the important fact: John L. Lewis
is known today as an evil man because his power
drives use organized labor rather than dollars, or
oil, or steel, for their furtherance. Labor, asking for
equality of power with capital and management, is
"the evil" that press and radio are out to throttle.
And John L. Lewis is shown up in the press for the
relatively immoral character he is, not in greatest
part because of his immorality of character, but in
the main because he — his name and his organization — stand as symbols for the aspiration and the
will of organized labor as it seeks an equality of
power with capitalist forces. I have little respect and
less admiration for "that *man*," John L. Lewis. But
for John L. Lewis, the symbol of organized labor
seeking to work out in our economic life some just
relationship between industrial wages and corporate
profits in relation to prices, I have a real, a vital, a
basic, sympathy.

Behind John L. Lewis, looming larger on the
national horizon than ever his name will, is this
problem which will not be settled by fines of labor
leaders and their unions for contempt of court as
they disregard injunction proceedings. Injunction
proceedings and fines will never solve the tussle between wage earner and profit takers as they jockey
for preferment in the field of changing prices. Such
methods will certainly complicate the problem by
adding heat to an already overheated issue which
really needs light. And the profit seekers and the
newspapers and some men in government are as

culpable in creating strike atmosphere and labor-capital tension as is John L. Lewis or any other labor leader standing as a symbol of labor in America.

Productive capital in America has a long, long history of excesses of which we have not seen the end. Labor has its excesses too — but fewer and shorter. According to the Federal Trade Commission report, issued at the end of the year (1946), the wholesale prices of manufactured goods during 1945-46 rose 23% to 25% more than the rise in the cost of production due to wage increases. The Federal Reserve Board for the second quarter of 1946 reports in a survey of six hundred industrial corporations that their average profits were 18% above the same wage period the previous year and 37% above the war years, 1942-45. Now, a 3% hourly wage increase raises wholesale production costs by 4%. A 10% profit increase might, therefore, be matched by a 30¢ to 50¢ per hour increase. But how many labor unions have asked that? And a 37% profit increase would have to be matched by a 50¢ to $1.00 per hour increase if increases in wages and profits were to advance proportionately.

Here are facts to ponder if you are interested in fairness and some kind of equality between capital and labor. And some capitalists are interested and some labor leaders are interested. But a great many are not. "John L. Lewis is responsible for the coal crisis!" The headlines howled it for weeks. "And are we going to fix him?" Answer by the columnists in almost unanimous choruses: "We are!" But did you notice during the last days of the coal strike, a little story in the local papers that Edward R. Burke,

President of the Southern Coal Producers representing management in the soft coal industry, was forced to resign his position as spokesman for the Southern Mine Owners? And why? Because he said publicly that he thought the miners should return to work, while at the same time the mine owners began negotiations with the miners' representative. Can it be, then, that when a man paid to represent the mine owners suggests negotiations (only that) based on the miners' demands, he gets fired? Apparently it can be. Apparently it happened to Edward Burke who lost a $30,000 job by merely suggesting that he talk the problem over with the leader of the miners. And that story of Burke's dismissal makes it plain to me that more people than John L. Lewis are responsible for the recent coal crises.

He brought the coal crisis to its end by losing his case. The owners refused to discuss publicly, much less to compromise. In the case of this last strike, they didn't have to. The government stepped in on the side of the public which also happened to be the side of the mine owners. But of course in the press, between the lines, the miners are villains for wanting enough money to buy one of those post-OPA, manna-from-heaven, high-priced beefsteaks for themselves and their kids.

The wild desire to continue the imbalance of power between capital and labor is further clearly indicated in a speech of Florida's own Attorney General, J. Tom Watson. Watson fronted the National Association of Manufacturers anti-closed shop amendment in Florida and with considerable help got it passed as law. On December 4, 1946, our Attorney General

stood before the Florida State Hotel Association and
urged those in attendance to "show that you have
some guts and fight together . . . refuse to recognize
any and all demands for a closed shop." And then
he backed his urging by legal threat, declaring that
he would bring "legal action" against anybody who
yielded to a labor demand for closed shop!

So, the picture of our Florida enforcer of justice
urging the Hotel Association to organize themselves
into a closed shop against any labor union that asked
for a closed shop! And if they should listen to a
closed shop demand by labor, he, by a law he helped
to legality, would prosecute them for breaking the
kind of closed shop which he advocates and enforces
for capital but denies to labor. This kind of pig-
headed one-sidedness makes me understand John L.
Lewis better. I cannot morally condone his methods.
But Tom Watson's speech certainly helps me understand why Lewis wants to use them. I will go further:
I can even understand that, perhaps not wanting to
use the methods he does, he finds no others which are
effective in getting even the semblance of social justice from the Tom Watsons in the U. S. A. Can you
understand this? If you can understand it then perhaps you too understand John L. Lewis as a symbol
of the aspirations of organized labor and why so
much is made of him. Understanding is a religious
exercise. I hope you will understand John L. Lewis,
the symbol, even though you do not very much like
"that man."

As for the coal crisis itself, that, in all probability
will outlast even John L. Lewis. I have a feeling that,
before it is settled in the public interest, it may be

necessary — in some plan like that advanced by Governor James M. Cox — to make another T.V.A. of the coal industry.

But that will be another story.

XII

AMERICA'S MOST INTOLERANT MAN

ON MARCH 12, 1947, Harry S. Truman, in his official capacity as President of the United States, issued an appeal to Congress which, in its long-run effect, may well turn out to be the first official call to arms for a third — and last — world war. Said the President, in asking for a four hundred million dollar appropriation to be used before June 30, 1948, for financial, material and military aid for Greece and Turkey: "This is no more than a frank recognition that totalitarian regimes imposed on free peoples, by direct or indirect aggression, undermine the foundations of international peace and hence the security of the United States." Mr. Truman further argued that: "The very existence of the Greek State is today threatened by the terrorist activities of several thousand armed men led by Communists."

To continue the presently constituted Greek and Turkish opposition to communism, the President asks for money. Now I am agreed with President Truman that "totalitarian regimes imposed on free people undermine the foundations of international peace and hence the security of the United States." In so far as the Soviet Union has perpetrated such regimes anywhere on earth, I agree with the President that the peace of the world is threatened. But, I am equally opposed to any such imposition of totalitarian or near-totalitarian regimes on any nation by Great Britain or by the United States. Such impositions of our force in places like Spain, China, the Dominican Republic or Puerto Rico, also places world peace and United States' security in jeopardy. Imposing our will on other nations endangers world peace and our security even if such an imposition is rationalized and propagandized as being made in the name of world peace and to promote domestic security.

Rationalizations do not constrict the workings of the President's well-stated principle. But the fact is that Mr. Truman's whole speech is directed to capitalizing on suggestions of the Soviet Union's violation of this principle in order to sharpen an appeal for funds to bolster up the shaky structures built on our own past Anglo-American violations. Mr. Truman's appeal for four hundred million dollars is based on the theory that Anglo-American friends are desirous of riding like White Knights to the rescue of a free people threatened by devils of communism.

But the fact is that Anglo-American conservative interests, according to the carefully respectable *New York Times* reports, first, re-armed reactionary Greeks to do battle against native Greek democrats, liberals and some Communists, and then after arranging such intimidation, gave the Greek people a right to vote for Communism or for reaction with no vital democracy allowed as an alternative. And the Greeks who voted, chose reaction in the form of monarchy, with many, in disgust, not voting at all.

President Truman's whole speech is based on the grand lie that the Greek people now have a democratic government and personnel of their own choos-

ing, when, in fact, the alternatives they were allowed
to vote on were virtually dictated, Anglo-American
alternatives. So, in fact, President Truman is now
asking for four hundred million dollars, a large part
of which is to rescue an increasingly weak, unpopular
and unworkable Anglo-American-sponsored Greek
government. Verily — to err is Truman!

Were this money to go for food, shelter, clothing,
medicine and machinery to benefit the Greek people
as a whole, as they need to be supported, we might
judge the President's plea as honest and in the interests of the Greek people. But, more than half the
funds asked for Greek "democracy" are to go to
build up Greek military forces under Anglo-American
tutelage. So it seems clear that the manipulated
Greek "democracy" is now to be financed with American money in order to rule by force of Anglo-American trained and supplied military force. A monarchy,
refurbished in London, backed by a military force
trained by Americans, is the "democracy" we are
asked to finance for Greece.

To have that loan approved by Congress, the
President displays great moral zeal in attacking the
mote in the eye of the Soviet Union; but he, with
equal care, refrains from mentioning the beam in the
Anglo-American eye. It is thus that a once dynamic,
democratic, liberal hope of political and economic
change for Greece is stifled and thwarted and
strangled near-to-death in the name of democracy
and freedom.

Moral self-righteousness on our part, an appli-
cation of Hitler's "big lie" theory and his "red bait-

ing" technique, are supposed to make us forget moral principles and facts in the case of Greece.

I hold no special brief for the Soviet Union or for Communism. I am not primarily interested in the Soviet Union; I am interested in honest facts and international justice. I am not primarily dedicated to furthering the ambitions of Anglo-American empire savers; I am interested in world peace.

Still, this fact grows clearer every day: Russian domination or Anglo-American domination is the fate which threatens most of the world's small nations. The end of that juggernaughting power-madness may well lead us, in fifteen or twenty years, over the precipice into World War III. The alternative is that the United Nations may grow in democratic spirit and method and strength into a genuine world government in which all nations, large and small, may have their co-operative and interdependent share of the freedoms, the wealth and the responsibilities of this earth.

But, the President of the United States has now dramatically rejected the United Nations and the World Bank as instruments of dealing with difficulties like those in Greece and Turkey, and at the very time when a UN organization is conducting an investigation of the Greek situation on the spot, he has chosen to back up the old methods of British imperialism in Greece and Turkey with American money. He has — unless the will of our people express itself strongly and soon — taken us a long step down the road that leads to World War III.

I have thus spoken about the crisis in the Mediterranean world, I have talked of Greece and Turkey

and the Dominican Republic and Spain and China because there is a situation developing in the United
States which is directly related to that in Greece.
More and more in the days ahead, we are going to
have to decide whether political democracy is valuable to us or not. We are going to have to decide
whether we are really interested in continuing to support the institutions of democracy: a free press, the
public school, freedom of belief, separation of church
and state, the right to vote, and the liberal spirit
which has nourished them. Greece may sound far
away from the United States; you may not think
that anybody will ever present you with two alternative forms of government from which to choose,
neither of them democracy! And yet, that is precisely the choice which has already been presented
to millions of people in this country.

On January 26, 1947, on a national radio network,
Reverend Fulton J. Sheen said: "From now on . . .
there will be no more half-drawn swords, no divided
loyalties, no broad strokes of sophomoric tolerance.
From now on men will divide themselves between
two religions . . . between the absolute who is the
God-man, and the absolute which is the man-God;
brothers in Christ, or comrades in anti-Christ."

Note it well! According to the theological authoritarianism of Fulton J. Sheen, from January 26, 1947
on, there can be no such thing as tolerance which he
calls "sophomoric." There can be only the undivided
loyalty with full-drawn swords on either side of a
battle between the ecclesiastical absolutism of Roman Catholicism and those who with it believe in
Jesus as Christ, and those on the other hand, whom

he calls anti-Christ and the devil.

See it now! There is no alternative, he declares, to an absolutistic supernaturalism or an absolutistic naturalism. Believe in Christ absolutely, or you have no alternative to being part of the absolutists in anti-Christ and co-workers of the devil.

And what, you may ask, becomes of the liberal spirit and the liberal institutions of democracy? In official pronouncements, published for all to read, such institutions as the public school, the free press, equal franchise, and freedom of conscience have been denounced by Roman Catholicism as "pestilential errors." But Reverend Fulton J. Sheen in his radio talks is more explicit and more bombastic. Chiding those who think that Roman Catholics believe in a red devil with a long tail, Sheen asks: "How will he (the devil) come in this new age to win followers. . . ?" His answer: "He will come disguised as the Great Humanitarian; . . . he will talk peace, prosperity and plenty, not as means to lead us to God, but as ends in themselves. He will write books on the new idea of God; . . . he will explain guilt away psychologically; he will spread the lie that men will never be better until they make society better; he will foster science; . . . he will foster more divorces under the disguise that another partner is 'vital'; he will invoke religion to destroy religion; he will even speak of Christ and say that he was the greatest *man* who ever lived; his mission, he will say, will be to liberate men from the servitudes of superstition and fascism, which he will never define; he will benevolently draw chocolate bars from his pockets for the little ones, and bottles of milk for the Hottentots. He will set up a counter church which will be the ape of the Church because, he the devil, is the ape of God."

Now from one point of view, Fulton Sheen is at least consistent. No one can reasonably accuse him in that description of the devil of being sophomorically tolerant. He is not tolerant; he is dogmatically intolerant. And you and I as Unitarians, and you and I as believers in the liberal principles and institutions of democracy, are the victims of his intolerance. You and I — we might as well face it now as later — are Reverend Fulton J. Sheen's "devil."

We have had the black shirt Mussolini as self-appointed denouncer of tolerance, progress and democracy; we have had the brown shirt Hitler, as fanatic a dogmatist and as great a persecutor of those who disagreed with him, as any the world has seen. In this country we have had our own night-shirted Ku Klux Klan to claim special authority for itself on the basis of its own brand of one hundred percent righteous superstitutions, and we have had a few silver shirts to sow seeds of divisiveness and hate.

But now comes a man, dressed in the purple shirt of ecclesiasticism, with a great landed aristocracy of wealth behind him, and a great aggregation of Catholic men to sponsor him on the radio in a weekly half-hour of authoritarian hate mongering; a man who alternately yells and whispers his intolerance of the liberal, democratic institutions which allow him his freedom to speak, deriding tolerance itself as sophomoric.

Now we have the official spokesman for the Catholic hierarchy trying to drive us all in fear and hate into the extreme right camp of clerical fascism or into the extreme left of Communism — assuring us all the while that liberalism, and by implication, democracy, is dead. So comes to these States, in a mighty panoply of power, Reverend Fulton J. Sheen, official spokesman for official Roman Catholicism, wearing his official purple shirt. And he is trying desperately to present to America the two alternatives with which little Greece was presented on a rigged slate of candidates. He is trying to tell us there is no tolerance; there is no liberalism; there is no democracy; there is only a purple fascism or red anti-Christ.

There is no red, white and blue any more. Red, white and blue is anti-Christ too. Red, white and blue is of the devil. Red, white and blue means "unity in diversity" — and he demands uniformity; Red, white and blue means "trial and error," and "majority rule" a "majority right" which he derides. He claims that only he and his church can be right or have the truth.

It is this same attitude of self-righteousness which he, and more than one of his brother prelates, has tried to sell, and is trying to sell: the Anglo-American world against the Soviet Union. And the newspapers — most of them — have for months re-echoed this self-righteousness against all of the bad — and against all of the good — attitudes and suggestions for world order made by the Soviet Union.

The President of the United States has caught the spirit of this same self-righteousness and expressed it recently in mouthings about our sending millions of dollars to Greece to keep that nation "free"! And again most of the press, in reporting that speech of

the President, continues to build up that self-righteousness against any and all suggestion of liberal, social change.

Tolerance in local affairs is "sophomoric"! Tolerance in international affairs is "sophomoric"! Now,
they say, it must be a drawn-sword battle between
purple fascism as one absolutism, and communism on
on the other hand.

I'll define purple fascism for Fulton J. Sheen! I'll
do more — I'll describe it for him. Purple fascism
was Austria under Dollfuss and Schuschnigg; purple
fascism was and is Spain under Franco; purple fascism is the end of liberal institutions, the death of free
speech, the persecution of dissenters against dog-
matism, the end of public schools, the blessing of
poverty as God's will! Purple fascism is a wealthy,
supernaturalistic church in league with a landed and
monied aristocracy to keep little people, poor people,
ignorant people, little poor, ignorant, and tied by fear
to the altars of a church which values its own creed
more highly than it values human lives.

Listen to Fulton J. Sheen again: I am but saying
in plain speech what he says in the symbolism of his
own authoritarian faith. "It is not so much a third
world war that is to be feared . . . as the coming of
. . . the Beast who will devour the child of the
Mother of Mothers." "The Beast" in his symbolism
stands for liberalism and democracy and communism
— all lumped together. And he says, in effect, that he
would rather have a third world war with all its fu-
tile horrors, death and starvation, than to have the
absolute faith in the Virgin Mary and her magical
son, Jesus Christ, changed or shattered. In that

statement we touch the motivation which leads Fulton J. Sheen to magnify his intolerance of liberal institutions and liberal values on the radio until it reaches five or ten or twenty million listeners each Sunday.

Fulton J. Sheen stands squarely across the path of democratic change in thought, word or deed. Fulton J. Sheen is trying to revive the middle ages of Catholic power and enlists all to this service whose first dedication is to *status quo* or to *status quo ante.* Fulton J. Sheen is deathly frightened for his weakening super-naturalistic faith, which he admits might be "devoured." He says that liberalism is dying. But don't be fooled by that statement of his, which is but his whistling in "the dark" he talks so much about. No Roman Catholic mouthpiece is going to stop work and buy expensive radio time just to conduct a requiem mass over the dead corpse of liberalism. Oh, no! Were liberalism dead, Fulton J. Sheen would never give radio time to its name. As it is, he is trying in his superstitious way to "put a hex on" liberalism, hoping that a declaration of death will result in actual death. Instead, I think he may find that liberalism will flourish under his vitriolic attacks.

Once, long ago, when the Jesuits held absolute power in Poland they drove out or massacred all liberal Unitarians. But liberalism and Unitarians are stronger now than they were then. And Fulton J. Sheen's church is weaker in the world now than it was then. No, I do not fear that liberalism will die or that social change will stop because Fulton J. Sheen expresses that hope in blasts of nation-wide radio-voiced intolerance. He may make himself the most powerfully intolerant man in America. But, I do not think that in the long run he will capture America, though he may breed intolerance against Roman Catholicism in America by his intolerance.

And so I charge you — keep it carefully in mind to distinguish between the spewers of hate in Roman Catholicism and some lovers of democracy who may be of that faith. Don't detest your Roman Catholic neighbors simply because those in power in that church have chosen to turn a bigot loose on us. Many of them will be as critical of "Father Sheen" as you are. Do not alienate such potential friends.

I have today tried to point out the real menace I see in the vitriolic expositions of the Reverend Fulton J. Sheen, who, despite some liberal spirit in American Catholicism, is striving to bring clerical fascism to this country. I have labelled his attempt, as it symbolizes other such, as purple fascism.

It is dangerous to us, a real and desperate short-run danger to democracy in this generation. Many in this day are trying to turn the clock of progress back to some one of their "good old days." Many non-Catholics are so striving. Indeed, radio-orator Sheen urges that all Protestants and all Jews who believe in his "absolutely true" ideas "of the moral law, the family, God, and the Divinity of Christ" join with him in prayerful unity. "If anti-Christ has his fellow travelers, then why should not God and his Divine Son?"

Protestants and Jews — unite with Roman Catholicism and its authoritarian ecclesiasticism as good and faithful fellow travelers! That, in effect, is the frank plea of the most arrogantly and powerfully intolerant man in America. That some Jewish and

Protestant organizations have already listened to that plea, I know to be a fact. That others have been threatened with boycott, and non-co-operation if they did not listen, I also know. That it is dangerous to personal security to use one's freedom in criticism, I also know.

Not long ago Pierre Van Paassen answered Fulton J. Sheen's first burst of radio intolerance as it was reported in *Time* magazine. Van Paassen's sermon in reply was also reported in *Time*. Immediately lecture engagements Van Paassen had made in various parts of the country began to be cancelled. The reaction to his criticism had set in. The swords of suppression were unsheathed and went to work on a lecturer and minister in this still somewhat free country. The Roman Catholic hierarchy will not burn Van Paassen at the stake to silence him as they would have certainly done to a critic a few generations ago, but they will make him pay for his criticism, and if they can they will silence him, just as they would keep every critic silent if they could.

This is no time to match hysterical intolerance with equal intolerance. But neither is it a time to hide our heads in the sands of our past democratic security. Democracy is not something to be put into archives like the copies of an old creed, nor yet something merely to be praised, saluted, or taken for granted. Democracy is the moving spirit of change in a diverse society which has decided to respect all its members. Democracy is the word that stands for a method of making social change peacefully. And fascism is the latest name we have given to the driving spirit of those who fight with violence against any and all social change — be it in theology, in politics, or in economics.

In his own great sermon, to which I have already referred, Pierre Van Paassen reported the story of a Nazi woman officer and her private torture methods in the Auschwitz concentration camp. This depraved female Nazi "took grotesque delight in being present in the maternity ward of the camp's hospital when Jewish women prisoners were about to be delivered and were suffering the first pangs of childbirth. That Nazi woman officer would then order leather straps to be fastened around the heels, the knees, the thighs, and the hips of the pregnant woman" who, therefore, could not bring forth the young body which struggled in her womb for light and life on earth. And mother and child strained, in this trussed up agony, until both perished a slow and horrible death.

All over the world new hopes, new values, new patterns of excellence struggle to be born, to grow, and to test their strength in life and society. And all over the world, in Central America, in South America, in Asia, Africa, and Europe the forces of hysterical reaction rush to buy straps to bind down the creative muscles of social change so that the new hopes may die in the womb of societies that struggle to give them birth. Puerto Rico, the Dominican Republic, Cuba, Brazil, Bolivia, Paraguay, Argentina, China, India, Indo China, Java, South Africa, Belgium, France, Spain, Italy, and Greece — these are but a few names to symbolize millions upon millions of hoping, struggling people.

Even in these States that struggle grows. I trust that change comes peacefully to the world and to the

United States. I trust a third alternative — democracy — works increasingly. But, if it does not, if creative forces, seeking change, are stifled and left to die by the orators and the armies of reaction, then, indeed, I should feel myself a traitor to the welfare of the humanity to which I seek to minister, did I not then with sword full drawn leap to cut the binding straps of progress.

Be that new born society fair of face and sweet to look upon, or be it a monster warped with suffering and hideous to behold, life at least would so be served, and the breath of real freedom. Nor do I doubt that in such circumstance each one of you would be found there beside me giving life to life, and in serving life so also serving hope which is forever prophetic of a better day for all the children of the earth.

XIII

CAN DEMOCRACY SURVIVE?

DEMOCRACY IS AN IDEAL and a political method. The best short statement of the ideal of democracy is Abraham Lincoln's "government of the people, by the people, for the people . . ." Yet, long before Lincoln made that cogent statement of the ideal of democracy, men who held it in their creatively revolutionary minds had succeeded in developing a political method which they believed made the achieve-. ment of that ideal possible. Under the republican form of government they created, a majority of the population by vote selected the leadership of the nation for a given period of time, two years, four or six, after which time the once chosen leadership either retired or took opportunity to stand for reelection.

Under this system of republicanism the right of the majority was automatically limited by the rights of minorities to educate and to agitate for change. In these States we say the majority is right. But if we know the tradition of our political method we are also bound to feel and to say that the majority is never more than right, that is, right at the moment; right until the next election; right, but never absolutely right. In the democratic spirit as written into the Constitution and Bill of Rights of this republic, the majority definition of the right is strictly limited by the minority's freedom to try by education and agitation short of violence to change previously approved definitions of the right. The glory of our republic is that it is such a form of self-government as not only recognizes social changes as fact, but makes possible the accomplishment of real change in the social process by orderly and peaceful methods.

For more than a hundred and fifty years the democratic spirit has found ample freedom for social change in this political method of constitutional government. For more than one hundred and fifty years this nation has defined and redefined its ideas of national right and welfare. While kingdoms fell and dictatorships sprang up and disappeared, the spirit and method of this democracy of ours has proved adaptable and creative for our use as a method of self-government. Its spirit is noble. In practice it has served us steadily and long. I believe in the democratic ideal and political method. I am dedicated to this method of persistent and peaceful social change by ballot. There is no better political ideal than government of, by, and for the people themselves.

But wise as were the founding fathers in giving substance in governmental form to that ideal by means of a Constitution and a Bill of Rights, that political method has not worked perfectly in achieving the democratic ideal. I truly believe that in most of the years of its life the people of this republic have had more power in self-government than have the peoples of any other nation on the globe. But they have never had complete control of their own government for their own sakes. They did not have it in the beginning. They do not have it now.

Listen: "Trifling as are the members of the Anti-Republican party, there are circumstances which give them an appearance of strength and numbers. They all live in cities together and can act in a body readily and at all times; they give chief employment to the newspapers and therefore have most of them under their command."

Those words were written in a day when the republican form of government was still considered in this country to be a fly-by-night, crack-pot experiment, promulgated by impractical dreamers and idealistic revolutionaries.

It was written in 1796 by a man who was standing solidly for the republican form of government and against those anti-republicans who in their unyielding devotion to monarchical and aristocratic nations were trying to sabotage and destroy a newborn democracy in a new world. It was Thomas Jefferson who observed that the anti-democratic forces of this country in 1796 had virtual control of the press and through it, he feared they might, one day, completely subvert popular government.

Here is a quotation from another president whom I think no one these days would call a revolutionary. A group recently visiting President Truman told him that the real estate lobby had a fund of ten million dollars to fight any and all legislation authorizing public housing. Said President Truman: "The lobby is always in a position to control legislation by spending a great deal of money to get out misinformation that deceives the public." Now, when a red-hunting President with many years of political experience behind him makes that kind of statement we are almost bound to believe him. Yet, how can lobbies with thousands or millions of dollars subvert the judgment of legislators and the populace to which they are responsibile and so effect legislative programs in their special interest and against the public welfare? President Truman says the lobbies are "always in a position" to do it. Taken at face value that must mean that in practice the democratic ideal is subverted by special interests in our nation so that descriptively it ought to be stated as government of all the people, by some of the people, for the sake of some of the people. President Jefferson was afraid for democracy. And apparently even President Truman is a little shocked at the degree to which special interests are subverting the democratic process to their special uses these days. Yet the question remains how can it be done? How can special interests buy special privilege at the public's expense? The statements of our Presidents Jefferson and Truman both point to one method of subversion: namely the misinformation of the public and by way of misinformation, the manipulation of the minds of people. But how do special economic interests manipulate the mind of an electorate so that it will sanction what is against the general economic welfare?

The great reporter Lincoln Steffens in his autobiography clearly sets forth many of the methods. Following Jefferson's clue, and from the inside, Steffens showed how newspapers shape and manipulate the public will for the sake of special economic groups. Jefferson said that the special interest groups "give employment to the newspapers and therefore have most of them under their command," and if one examines the interlocking special interests of newspapers and radio ownership with that of large producers and distributors in this nation, it is easy to understand that what Jefferson saw in his day is even truer on a much larger scale today. The growth of the power of special interests is one of the things that Lincoln Steffens describes in his autobiography. The corporations in America began their drive for controlling power back before the horse-car days. First in the local community, then in the state, then in the nation and now all over the world. The corporations which glorify private competition in speech and press have persistently sought to achieve economic monopoly in practice, and with their power actually achieved on any level have sought political control as a way of guaranteeing and extending continued economic control.

Local horse-car companies strove mightily to drive out competitors by seeking the election to office of those men in a city who would agree in advance to produce after election a monopoly contract to run the horse-cars in that city. With a monopoly in horse-car service thus granted, the owner's profits were guaranteed whether good or bad service was thereafter in effect. Most of our fairly large corporations are great supporters of "free competition," for by means of it they hope to create monopolies for themselves in their fields of endeavor. That's why they are for it. In this respect they are like those authoritarian political and ecclesiastical groups in the world which are strong in their advocacy of freedom. "Freedom" is the means toward their unspoken totalitarian purposes.

Now, magnify the 1860 horse-car monopoly in a
city of one hundred thousand people to the large national and international companies of our day, and
you get some idea of the special galaxies of power
which are now arrayed against truly popular rule.
Now national laws are written or erased by special
interest groups fighting singly or in loose-jointed co-
operation. Each tries to have its own man elected
to Congress in Washington. In this effort local edi-
torial "friends" of local papers and radio stations are
enlisted.   Once in Washington, house and senate
committee hearings are "arranged." Newsworthy
"friends" are cajoled or employed to testify for a
desired bill or against an undesirable measure. High-
powered public relations experts are employed to do
the "arranging" and to expedite news reporting and
news handouts and feature stories. Since most of
the large newspapers and radio chains are themselves
part of the growing constellation of interrelated special interests, nobody has to *buy* much help. During
three generations of corporation drive for economic
monopoly the special economic interest groups are
cleverly and compactly organized to manipulate the
public will. Thus, recently, against the public interest (it is now clear and will be clearer in the days
ahead) price ceilings and control were so maligned,
testified against, and struck at by the vast powers of
large corporations, that the people themselves after
two years of publicity barrage, were converted to a
hatred of their O.P.A. O.P.A. was killed, and by
educated "popular" demand. Behind that demand
was a vast army of carefully organized and highly

paid representatives of American big business who had arranged and conditioned it.

Now, here is the stark, direct question: can democracy survive the attacks of the power-seeking economic interests which are more and more intent and able to subvert it for their own selfish profit? Quite frankly, I do not know the answer to that question. But I do know that it is rapidly becoming the crucial question to our nation. The survival of political democracy is the critical question not merely because economic cliques have always, and are now in larger degree than ever before, subverting government of, by and for the people. Democratic survival is a serious question today because the planners of the monopoly-seeking corporations, which have long thwarted the full functioning of our republican form of government, in recent years know themselves and their individual and corporate economic aims to be threatened by an alternative economic ideal.

In the past political democracy has certainly been a stumbling block in the way of special economic interests seeking monopolistic powers. Not even the best and biggest people can fool all the people all the time. Yet today, monopoly-seeking capitalists are faced with the rapidly growing alternative economic ideal of planned production and distribution of material abundance.

Now the ideal of monopoly-capitalism is a planned relative scarcity of material goods for the sake of high and stable profits. To the monopoly-capitalist who has been willing and able to subvert political democracy to achieve his economic ends, the idea of planning the production and distribution of economic

plenty seems, to put it in one word, "Communism"!
If you really want to know what the label-pasters
mean these days by "Communism" here it is. "Communism" is the word that monopoly-minded adver-
tising and public relations men use to warn all minds
away from the ideal of the planned creation and use
of material plenty. In these minds the Soviet Union
stands as the prime symbol of a nation at work striving to achieve this economic ideal. And not far behind
the Soviet Union in fitting their use of the word was
Franklin Delano Roosevelt in some aspects of the
New Deal. This is the reason the New Deal was
hated and vilified in the late 1930's and early 1940's
by the very men who profited most from it; this is
the reason the red-baiting campaign of 1947 now
blows so hot. Some New Dealers did try by a little
planning to produce and to distribute plenty. The
Tennessee Valley Authority is a small example of
trying to produce and to distribute electricity in an
area. The Soviet Union, under Communist government, with regular intervals of economic planning
is attempting to produce and distribute enough for
all its citizens. And therefore it is charged that anybody is "Communist" who believes we have the po-
tentialities in machinery and material and planning
genius to wipe out scarcity in America.

Look you! Who is it in the United States that
speaks loudest against the authoritarian New Deal,
against the authoritarian Russians? Who is it pleads
longest in the press, and on the radio not to give up
our democratic way of life in favor of Russian Communism? Why it is the very kind of people who for
one hundred and fifty years have subverted political

democracy for the sake of cultivating their own special privileges. Have they cherished political democracy in the past? They have not. Do they cherish it now? They do not. They are asking us to hate Communism in order to make us hate the benefits that "communism" and a "planned economy" have in common. They are ready and willing to kill political democracy in order to retain all hopes of monopolistic economic control.

Why did Thyssen finance Adolf Hitler? To save the Weimar Republic from the dictatorship of the proletariat? Bah! Thyssen and hundreds of his kind, in Germany, Holland, Britain and the United States financed Hitler for the ultimate death of political democracy, the hope of realizing economic monopoly, and the destruction of the ideal of economic plenty which was clearest symbolized in the political ideal behind the government of the Soviet Union.

Let one of the loudest spokesmen for the vested interests in America tell you this himself. In the *Los Angeles Tidings* Fulton J. Sheen recently published this parable, "Just suppose a small village of five hundred souls had no burglars in it; that is there would be no lock on any door. Now imagine one burglar bent on violence entering that town: five hundred locks would have to be put on the doors of five hundred homes. Now suppose that the Communists enter not a town of five hundred, but a nation. Some kind of lock must be made to keep them out, and the lock which is presently made in most countries of the world is "Fascism!"

The lock which is presently made is Fascism! We

have already seen that the ideals of monopoly-capitalism move men to plan to retain and to enforce relative economic scarcity. And we have also discovered that monopoly-capitalists quite generally label anybody who believes in the ideals of planned economic plenty a communist. I myself have been so labelled by many people for believing in that idea. So, from the late President Roosevelt on down there have been and are hundreds of thousands of people in this country whom Fulton J. Sheen and others of his economic view would be delighted to label "Communists."

"Communists" of this sort are scattered all over this country. They backed the New Deal by the millions for twelve years, but unfortunately are not organized in any way except the democratic process of voting. But they are here—this kind of "communist" the monopoly-capitalists are striving to make powerless in their voting privileges. For in the regular fashion of democratic voting they threaten, as a thief threatens an icebox. They threaten to "steal" away the usurped power of the old controllers of economic scarcity who have long subverted the full workings of political democracy. And Fulton J. Sheen has made his decision as to how to deal with these "thieves" who in constitutional manner would recapture their economic freedom. The lock against such people which is presently made is Fascism. . . . Is it "totalitarianism," Sheen and his ilk are afraid of in these United States? Is it political democracy he and his fellow travelers would defend?

Fascism is Sheen's weapon against those who, in the regular workings of political democracy, as in republican Spain, might some day vote for a planned economic plenty. To prevent the planning of eco-nomic democracy for our nation there are amongst us today thousands of persons with millions of dollars at their command who would willingly kill political democracy! And because the country has in it other millions with hopes for economic plenty, the fears of the monopoly-minded in business and church and government are rapidly mounting, until they are breaking out, openly, in sympathetic understanding of the killing function of fascism.

Why is it that we impose or approve fascist or near-fascist leaders in Europe, Asia and South Amer-ica? Basically, I think it is because those who con-trol our government are afraid that if they allowed those peoples to have the political democracy they say they believe in and cherish, those people would take advantage of their political democracy to vote in a so-called "leftist" economy with provisions for planning national plenty. Those who presently con-trol our government can't trust people with full po-litical democracy—not even in the U.S.A. Therefore they manipulate the public will in America against its own interests; therefore they give Greece a king to vote for, finance a dictatorship in Turkey, keep fasc-ists going in Spain and China and hold South Ameri-can rightists in dictatorial power against the mount-ing hopes of an aspiring people.

In our day there are two revolutionary ideals that move men and women to action. One of them, the ideal of political democracy, was born in revolution at the time of the formation of the United States of America. The other dynamic ideal the goal of production and distribution of economic plenty by means of planning, was born full-blown with the Russian revolution of 1917. And those two ideals are increasingly capturing the minds and hearts and wills of people all over the earth. Neither ideal is fulfilled, yet both remain dynamic.

I do not mean that the Soviet Union is going to send its agents to the United States, to South America, to China and Africa to advance the ideal of planned plenty. Soviet representatives are stationed in most of the countries of the world—as are ours. But I am sure that theirs are not organizing economic revolution, as I am sure we are not planning politically democratic revolution. But these two revolutionary ideals live on in every nation on earth. We in the United States can kill our political democracy, but the ideal will still live. The Soviet Union does not have to send out organizing agents to work for economic change for that ideal is alive all over the world. All they have to do is to make that ideal of economic democracy work reasonably well in their own country, as we have tried in the United States to make political democracy work reasonably well. A revolutionary leader whose thinking I greatly admire has stated the principle clearly and forcibly. I trust his statement for its truth and soundness. "A . . . solid . . . government maintained here will be a standing monument and example for the aim and imitation of the people of other countries; and I join in the hope and belief that the inquiry which has been excited among the mass of mankind by our Revolution and its consequences will ameliorate the condition of man over a great portion of the globe."

That quotation, an excellent statement, I think, of Stalinism, was made by the revolutionist Thomas Jefferson, just a few weeks before he became the third President of the United States.

And while we are comparing the two great revolutionary ideals of our time it might be well to recall that on July 14, 1791, as a result of participating in a celebration of the fall of the Bastille in France, given by the Constitutional Society of Birmingham, England, Joseph Priestly, scientist and Unitarian minister who sympathized with the ideals of both the American and French Revolution, had his chapel burned to the ground and his home sacked by a mob, though he managed to escape to America with his life.

The ideal of political democracy is a dangerous and a contagious ideal. Thousands of people were willing to do violence to its advocates—thousands are still willing to do violence to subvert it. And there are thousands today who would be willing if not indeed eager to do violence against the ideal of planned production and distribution. Fear that in the democratic process the majority of people will vote for a planned economy may lead the minority to destroy our republican form of government by the violence of fascism.

Authoritarianism is no practical threat to democracy, except from reaction! But even that need not necessarily happen. To my knowledge Bernard M. Baruch, frequent presidential advisor, has not yet been denounced as Communist. Yet in a recent statement he urged that during the next twenty-one months no employer should lay off an employee, no union should call a strike, but that the productive plants of this country should operate to capacity on a forty-four hour week. That is Mr. Baruch's twenty-one month plan. It is not a "five year plan" it is true, but it is more than a third of the way toward one. Who knows, perhaps the ideal of political democracy may yet reinforce and be reinforced by the ideal of planned economic production and distribution for the common good.

Maybe democracy and communism are closer together in practice than the label pasters think. Maybe indeed they are no farther apart than the monopoly-capitalists fear. Whether the two great nations which symbolize these two revolutionary ideals of economic and political democracy can come closer together in co-operation and so avoid war is of course, in part up to the government and people of the Soviet Union. But in equal part it is up to our government and our people.

Co-operation and peace is a two way street. How shall we walk on our side? In traditional devotion to democratic ideals? Or in ways which lead to fascism?

XIV

THE END OF THE WORLD

REPENT YE! The end of the world draws nigh!

Change your hearts! Change your motives!
Change your attitudes! Change your values! Change
your way of life!

The kingdom of God is at hand!

That was the admonition of Jesus of Nazareth.
That was the fervor and the fire of Jesus' religion.
That was the appeal of his preaching: the world is
coming to an end! Prepare now, to live in the kingdom of God that is to come!

What did Jesus mean by "the end of the world"?
Most people nowadays, including "Jehovah's Wit-
nesses," who claim they teach just as he did, are inclined to think that Jesus believed that the earth itself was going to be destroyed along with all the
people on it, by an angry God. Only the elect, only
the believer, only the followers of Jesus were to be
saved, and their salvation was to be achieved in
spirit only, in another, heavenly, world.

Maybe such an interpretation of Jesus' teaching
concerning the end of the world is right. Certainly
later Christians claimed their "kingdom of heaven"
was Jesus' "kingdom of God," but personally I doubt
it. I doubt such literalist interpretations precisely because I am convinced that Jesus was no literalist himself. The Pharisees were literalists, "the blind lead-
ing the blind," and Jesus excoriated them. I doubt

this literal interpretation of "the end of the world" as meaning the destruction of the earth. I doubt the interpretation of a coming kingdom as meaning a kingdom in heaven after the earth be destroyed.

Jesus was at once more practical in his religion and less literal than most of the literalists who have tried to understand him. I am convinced that Jesus, in the best tradition of the highly ethical Hebrew prophets, looked about him in his day, and on the basis of his applied ethical principles, judged calmly that the social world in which he lived was simply too rotten morally to survive. Ethical religion is first of all an admonition for life, teachings which make for social survival and growth in spiritual and physical terms. And when those ethical principles are broken, death—social and personal, death—results. And Jesus, as he beheld the individuals scrambling for preferment, the disregard of personal life, the ruthless economic exploitations, the substitution of violence for the rule of moral forces as a way of social control, the heartless dictator vying for power, the moral lethargy and general hopelessness of the body politic, the failure of outmoded and self-seeking religious institutions to impart a creative and life-giving direction to personal and social life, as Jesus beheld all these and countless other symptoms of social decay, he concluded that society, the creative interrelation of man in his day, was cracking up, approaching its end of social usefulness to human life, and would go down through chaos into the limbo of forgotten civilizations.

Of course they called him "as silly as a wine-bibber," all those Roman Quislings, all those careful, comfortable keepers of the letter of the law, all those enjoyers of privilege and power.

But some people listened to him, people whose spiritual world was barren and bleak. And all alike, doubters and believers, asked him, "When shall these things be? What shall be the sign of the end of the world?"

And then he gave his evidences, such as they could understand. He said: "Many shall come in my name saying, I am Christ, and shall deceive many. And ye shall hear of wars and rumors of wars: see that ye be not troubled: for all these things must come to pass, but the end is not yet. For nation shall rise against nation, and kingdom against kingdom: and there shall be famines . . . in divers places. All these are the beginning of sorrows." [1]

"Brother shall betray the brother to death, and the father the son; and children shall rise up against their parents, and shall cause them to be put to death." [2] "And then shall many . . . betray one another, and shall hate one another." [3] "The love of many shall wax cold." [4] "Woe unto them that are with child, and to them that give suck in those days! But pray ye that your flight be not in winter. . . . For then shall be great tribulation, such as was not since the beginning of the world to this time." [5] "Then if any man shall say unto you, Lo! here is Christ, or there; believe it not. For there shall arise false Christs and false prophets, and shall

---

[1] Matthew, 24: 5-8.
[2] Mark, 13: 12.
[3] Matthew, 24: 10.
[4] Matthew, 24: 12.
[5] Matthew, 24: 19-21.

show great signs and wonders; . . . they shall deceive the very elect. Behold, I have told you before." [6] "This generation shall not pass till all these things be fulfilled. Heaven and earth shall pass away, but my words shall not pass away. But of that day and hour knoweth no man!" [7]

That in general was Jesus' answer to those who asked about the coming of the end of the civilization of his time. You can read it all and much more in your New Testament. No, Jesus couldn't tell precisely the hour or the day that the Roman-dominated Graeco-Mediterranean world would collapse. But he did know that when most people distrust most other people, that when most nations are engaged in bloody tests of violence, that when starvation is rampant, that then social decay has set in as the prelude to cultural death.

The most interesting, by far the most significant thing for us about Jesus' teaching concerning the end of a social world, is that it turned out, as he predicted, to be true. Jesus' world, the Graeco-Roman cultural world, did come to an end. Even now, after it is history, we cannot say precisely the hour or the day or the year, that it happened. There is in history, however, many a treatise concerning the "decline and fall of Rome." Jesus lived in the moral decline of that Empire, which preceded the decline of creativeness and the decline of power.

Power, brute force, the power to hold on, the power to survive, the power to kill, goes last in a culture. Moral force goes first, creativeness goes

---

[6] Matthew, 24: 23-25.
[7] Matthew, 24: 34-36.

second, but without ethical base and creative direction, power, however great, however destructive,
puffs out its last death-dealing energy and dies. So
Roman power died, as Jesus saw it would, for lack
of a creatively ethical base to stand upon. And even
a scientist, especially a scientist, who works for
theories which give him knowledge for prediction,
should admire the insight into life which enabled
Jesus of Nazareth to foretell that the end of his
world was at hand, and to plan a new society to take
the place of the old—the kingdom of God.

On the basis of clear and certain evidence, Jesus
saw it: the destruction of the old, the creation of the
new. And today, on the basis of evidence no less
clear, and equally certain, I say to you:

Repent! Change your hearts! Change your motives! Change your attitudes! Change your values!
Change your way of life! For the end of our world
is at hand.

Do you want signs or proof that it is so? Then
look at the western world. Since Martin Luther
drove the first wedge into the tarnished armor of
the Roman Catholic Church, scholastic theology,
upon which that religion was based, has continued to
rust and rot away in the face of a skeptical Protestant and scientific rain of doubts and facts. Protestantism itself, which in the sixteenth, seventeenth
and eighteenth centuries laid a new moral ground for
the culture of the west, has been unable to survive
the moral nihilism of scientific agnosticism. For a
hundred years past, Protestantism has failed as a
creative ethical agent. For a century the machine has
been haloed with a dollar and worshipped as God

incarnate, the new savior. And even now, blood and sinew, human blood and sinew, is hourly pressed into the hungry maw of the machine, a living sacrifice made in exchange for a few really useful gadgets, a torrent of ten-cent-store trinkets, and a flood of machines to make more machines to make new and bigger and more efficient instruments of death and destruction.

In the Orient the old religions have long lain sodden in decay. For centuries past, the holiest man of the east was one who would renounce his own desireful, potentially creative life, in favor of a living death by beggary. Now we have sold his children the machine, and they, too, pour themselves more and more into it. Japan, which has now exchanged its old religious desireless character for the new gadget and its use, gives a fairly clear indication of what western civilization, so-called, may do for the so-called backward peoples of Asia, once we really get them fully converted to the religion of power. Hardened to death by their dying religions, they should be artists in dealing death, once the machine has fully "tooled them up" as war-makers. The old religions, then, fail, and will fail to furnish moral base and creative direction for a world society.

The religion of machine production in capitalistic competition, must, by its very nature, produce strife, and does so; a strife which periodically breaks out on a Gargantuan scale in war. And as the scale of the strife continues, the vastness and the destructiveness of the wars enlarges. "Peace in our time" has become merely another phrase with which to describe the next war's preparation.

So now, after World War II has reached its dramatic climax, the loot is being stored away, the land and sea bases are already being consolidated, to make it possible for fewer and fewer nations to fight a larger war of destruction. The principle of self-determination for little nations, which we say is one of the ethical principles for which the war is fought, becomes less and less of a reality with each new victory on each new front. The delivery of "Four Freedoms" to anybody in the world becomes less and less likely, with each fiery blast of high-powered artillery and each new shower of bombs. The Russian Ukraine cannot possibly be rebuilt, even in its old shoddiness, in ten years. Italy cannot regain for fifteen or twenty years in physical equipment alone, what she had under the Fascist stooge, Mussolini. Large areas of the Balkans may not be rebuilt in a generation, even if the will to build replaces the fear of war and the will to destruction which now pervades the world.

The fear is too great. The will to build is too weak. Capital is too fearful to venture, unwilling to lose its life as of old, robustly, creatively. And national interest is imperialistic and aggressive.

The good neighbor ideal is a hangover wish out of the best of the Christian faith, applied to international relations because of immediate fear of an enemy across the sea; but even then, in the face of deep fear, it is applied mostly in newspaper headlines.

The Nazi analysis of the democratic nations is unfortunately more true than most of us care to admit. The chief Nazi mistake, and one which we increasingly share with them, is in supposing that a community can be built on physical force and the threat or use of violence. The Nazis tried to build a United States of Europe on that basis, after our moral creativeness in the shape of Woodrow Wilson's plea proved insufficient to build it a better way. Our moral creativeness was too weak for the job, and failed, resting as it did on the base of dying religious institutions. And the Nazi method of armed violence failed to unite Europe because it could not win the hearts of men, whatever it did to their bodies.

Brute power, however strong, will always fail to create community; always, it engenders hatred, disunity, dissolution, even as it courts counterviolence. The Nazi attempt to unite Europe by the sword has perished by the sword. Our attempt to organize the world by the sword will also perish by the sword.

Order, community, society, rests on the moral assent of trusting souls: moral will, reinforced maybe with a few words. But to expect moral order to be created in society by violence applied from above or from outside, is to expect the moon to shine bright as the sun.

And because our leaders and the peoples of the world generally have in such large part lost this central ethical principle, our age is doomed.

"Nation shall rise against nation, and kingdom against kingdom," and empire against empire. Yes — even America — "shine perishing republic fast hardening to Empire!"

"And there shall be famines in divers places!" Well, we have got past that stage of disintegration when we expect to hear rumors of wars. Nation *has* risen against nation: the first world war a generation ago, the second world war today, the third world war and maybe a fourth. It is all one war, fought in the name of perishing life-giving ideals, but in the method that can lead but to one end only: the end of civilization, the end of our world. The moral spirit, the creative spirit of our civilization, is dying of malnutrition. What more natural than that bodies should also be starving?

Not long ago I read of a Chinese woman who was haled into court for eating her infant. She asked to be excused of the crime. The baby, she said, was already dead of starvation.

Last week I was told by a soldier back from Europe, that he once saw a youngster of nine or ten years start whittling at the leg of a frozen corpse, seeking food.

Shocked? Horrified? At the end of the world we are helping to bring to Europe and Asia?

Of course we are. Most of us. America is still an ivory tower where decay has not yet reached the height of full-powered madness, let alone destruction.

In the next war we will share starvation and haunting hatred with all the world. Yes, even now, in our midst, the insane moral perversion is already among us. Isn't it significant that Henry Wallace, whose "love of the many" is as real and as publicly spoken as anyone's anywhere in the world, should himself be able in practice to feed the starving multitude by no better method than by ploughing up wheat, burning oranges, and killing little pigs? And even he, watered down and perverted as were his ideals by the exigencies of political and economic practice, struggles now against public rejection.

An immoral world, a power-mad world, a decaying world, a death-dealing world, a starving world, a mad world . . . rushing to self-destruction!

That is why, that is how, our world cultures are coming to an end. Ethical debility, power-madness, destruction of war, all ending in starvation, insanity and disease, will bring our world to its end.

When brother betrays brother, and child sacrifices parent, and parents betray one another and their children, then you may know that the end is nigh. That is community spirit broken to pieces. I saw it and felt it in Europe, where for ten years it has consistently happened. I can feel it coming here, and so can you, you liberals, who are already careful, distrustful of your fellows when you speak. Wherever you go, that feeling, that suspicion, that fear, that mounting hatred, that individualism to which we are reduced without higher goal than self, without deeper roots than bodily sensation, that aloneness of spirit; that is the feel of a society breaking up. That is the experience of a world culture coming to an end.

One more major war will, I think, complete the destruction. A war between the east and the west, fought with robot bombs. A war between the right and the left, going on inside and between nations ought to complete it. And that war, if I am any moral judge of our day, is very probable.

For ten years before this second stage of the world war, many of us worked to prevent it by advocating, everywhere we could, that collective security be maintained in a league of morally-bound nations with force behind them.

But moral regeneration in world terms was not achieved. Moral lethargy and decay, coupled with love of and belief in power, brought the war. We continue to work for a world organization of co-operating and no longer sovereign nations, based on their own moral assent and backed up by an international police force. I will work for that world organization until the third phase of this world war comes, as I hope it never comes.

But this is clear. War must end in the world, or civilization will end in war.

My present conviction is and has been for several years, that warring groups of people may destroy what we now know as civilization. Two wars have taken us far in that direction already. Our civilization, east and west, is not sufficiently ethical in its own inner convictions, in its practices, to survive. The end of the world is at hand.

Twelve years ago, in a New Testament class, an old, brilliant scholar and student of Jesus' life and times, gave me an insight into what Jesus meant by the end of the world and the coming of the kingdom of God. For at least half that many years, I have been trying almost consciously to keep from seeing the implications of Jesus' principles and observation for our chaotic day. But the insight persisted. Much study and world events have deepened and sharpened it. Our civilization *is* coming to an end. "Of that day and hour knoweth no man," no, not even of that year, or of that generation, do we know exactly.

But of this I am convinced. We live amidst moral

and social decay and violent disintegration. We live at the end of our old world-order. Yet somehow, amidst the decay and chaos of our society, it is our duty to build the fabric of a new world to come. Even as the old world comes to a violent, evil death, a vitally ethical and creative religion must be born, which will help us lift up our battered heads and seek for ourselves, for our fellows, and for the future, a better way of life, out of which may finally appear a world religion and a world order for all mankind.

XV

THE LIBERAL LOOKS AT THE CROSS

I HAVE SEEN IT shining on the white heights of Sacre
Coeur in Paris. I have seen it emblazoned in jewels
on the crown of a long-dead king. I have seen it em-
broidered in gold on the vestments of a venerable
bishop. I have seen it squatly bright above an onion
spire in Oberammergau. I have seen it cheaply gilded
on a shoddy parish church on the prairies of Minne-
sota. I have seen it shining in the resplendence of a
thousand lighted candles in a mission church of New
Mexico. I have seen it spotlighted in golden glow
in a modern English cathedral. I have seen it carved
in stone on the tomb of an ancient crusader. I have
seen it dangling like an enchanting spell on the
breasts of young maidens. I have seen it on a deli-
cate chain hung as a beneficent gold charm on the
necks of babies. I have seen the cross of gold, symbol
of Christianity.

The gilded cross, the bejeweled cross, the shining
cross, is a symbol of a religious theology. And it
tells a story. It tells us that Adam and Eve, our
"first parents," committed the sin of disobedience to
God; that since their sin all humanity is born in sin.
It tells us that human beings, "sinners," are completely incapable in themselves or of themselves to
save themselves. But further the gilded cross tells us
of God's mercy to men; how seeing their hopeless sin-
fulness God sent Christ, His only begotten son, to

suffer and to die for all sinners, that His anger might be appeased, that His heart might be softened, that through the shed blood of a suffering and dying Christ they might be redeemed and so enter into the bliss of an eternal life in heaven. Through the suffering of Christ on the cross, through the shedding of his blood, the punishment of human sin is remitted by God as atoned for by His only son. "Washed in the blood" of Christ, humanity is spared the eternal wrath of God. The cross then is forgiveness. The cross is hope of heaven. The cross is personal salvation. Therefore do Christians regard the cross so highly. Therefore do they gild the cross, bejewel the cross, place the cross on the pinnacle of their buildings. Therefore do they wear it around their necks. Therefore do they think to bless themselves by making the sign of the cross upon their bodies. "In the cross of Christ" they "glory." It is their "key to heaven."

So it is that Christians plead with us to "come to" their cross. They exhort us to "accept" the cross. They threaten damnation to us if we reject the cross, and heaven, if we believe on their cross.

Carl Sandburg was not precisely just to the orthodox Christians when he wrote his "Lines to a Contemporary Bunk-Shooter." Indeed, he was not thinking about justice for Christian theologians. Rather was he thinking about being just to Jesus, the man of Galilee, as with delicious anger at the insidious mockery which the gilded cross of Christianity makes of the man who died on Golgotha's height, he excoriates the magic mongers who shout their faith in Christ as the Savior. Says Sandburg: "You come

along . . . tearing your shirt . . . yelling about Jesus.
Where do you get that stuff? What do you know
about Jesus? Jesus had a way of talking soft and
outside of a few bankers and higher-ups among the
con-men of Jerusalem, everybody liked to have this
Jesus around because he never made any fake passes
and everything he said went and he helped the sick
and gave the people hope. You come along squirting
words at us, shaking your fist and calling us all damn
fools so fierce the froth slobbers over your lips . . .
always blabbing we're all going to hell straight off
and you know all about it. I've read Jesus' words. I
know what he said. You don't throw any scare into
me. I've got your number. I know how much you
know about Jesus. He never came near clean people
or dirty people, but they felt cleaner because he came
along. It was your crowd of bankers and business
men and lawyers who hired the sluggers and the
murderers who put Jesus out of the running. I say
the same bunch backing you nailed the nails into the
hands of this Jesus of Nazareth. He had lined up
against him the same crooks and strong-arm men now
lined up with you, paying your way. This Jesus was
good to look at, smelled good, listened good. He
threw out something fresh and beautiful from the
shine of his body and the touch of his hands wherever
he passed along. You slimy bunk-shooter, you put a
smut on every human blossom in reach of your rotten
breath belching about hellfire and hiccupping about
this man who lived in Galilee. When are you going
to quit making the carpenters build emergency hos-
pitals for women and girls driven crazy with wrecked
nerves from your gibberish about Jesus. — I put it

to you again: Where do you get that stuff; what do you know about Jesus? You tell people living in shanties Jesus is going to fix it up all right with them by giving them mansions in the skies — after they're dead and the worms have eaten 'em. You tell six-dollar-a-week department store girls all they need is Jesus; you tell poor people they don't need any more money on pay day and even if it is fierce to be out of a job, Jesus will fix it up alright, all right — all they gotta do is take Jesus the way you say. I'm telling you Jesus wouldn't stand for the stuff you're handing out. Jesus played it different. The bankers and lawyers of Jerusalem got their sluggers and murderers to go after Jesus because Jesus wouldn't play their game. He didn't sit in with the big thieves. I don't want a lot of gab from a bunk-shooter in my religion. I've been to this suburb of Jerusalem they call Golgotha where they nailed him, and I know, if the story is straight, it was real blood ran from his hands and the nailholes. And it was real blood spurted in red drops where the spear of the Roman soldier rammed in between the ribs of this Jesus of Nazareth."

Do you see what I mean when I say that Carl Sandburg doesn't think much of the theory that Jesus came down, from heaven to earth, by direction from God to make a sinning populace happy about a cross of gold which they could cherish as salvation? Carl Sandburg may not be a theologian. He may not be quite just to Christian theologians. But you must admit he does have the seeing eye and the compassion of a poet's soul for people, even for the man Jesus. And he is healthily impatient of cant and magic mongering and hypocrisy. The milk of human sym-

pathy has not curdled in him. He knows a man when
he sees one: and he speaks out for that man and
against the treacherous hope which for centuries has
made us think of Jesus, not as a person, but as a
tool with which to pry open the gates of heaven.

Why, oh why, must greatness always be betrayed
by blind self-seeking littleness? "Consider greatness.
. . . No man standing alone has ever been great except, most rarely, his will, passion, intellect, have
come to posthumous power and the naked spirit
picked up a crown. Yes, alas then, poor ghost
Nietzsche or Jesus, hermit, martyr, or starved
prophet, were you honest while you lived? You are
not now. You have found your following and it cor-
rupts you. All greatness, involves betrayal — of the
people by a man — or of a man by the people."

Robinson Jeffers is right. All greatness involves
betrayal: "of the people by a man" (think of Hitler),
"of a man by the people" (think of Buddha, Socrates
— think of Jesus). In the Garden of Gethsemane
Jesus might have betrayed his followers and his own
convictions. He might have lied to Pilate and escaped
with his life. He chose to stick by his convictions
and his followers. Jesus betrayed nobody. But his
followers betrayed him; they have done it for centuries, and are still doing it. Jesus came bringing
hope of a better world, "a more abundant life" for
men in the here and now. Jesus, the liberal among
conservatives, was, and is, betrayed. He was betrayed
by a self-seeking Judas into the hands of his enemies.
He was betrayed by his most intimate disciples and
hung at last — a convict — on rude crossed planks
of splintery wood. A Jewish Sacco or Vanzetti of

the long ago, he was victim of the fear and rage of an incited multitude. And afterward he was betrayed by the neurotic, hopeful wishes of his disciples who in their need conjured him up amongst them, "resurrected," for a sign of their own survival after death. And then the theologians betrayed the man Jesus, betrayed him to make a profitable shortcut, betrayed him for their own sakes, betrayed him in favor of a sacramental springboard into heaven, sold out Jesus the man in favor of Christ the Son of God.

So was Jesus' life emasculated. His work was beclouded. His death, his convict's death on a rude cross, was tinseled with selfish hope, and the cross itself, the harsh wooden cross, was gilded. It stands today as a symbol of the final rejection of the facts of Jesus' glorious life and his ignominious death. The gilded cross is an ancient hopeful lie that men have been telling themselves about the life of a prophetic Jew whom they still betray.

Jesus' real life — what was it? It was the life of a religiously unconventional Jew lived under harsh Roman dictation and suppression. He loved his own people but he loved other peoples also. He was more unafraid than most to love, more courageous than most to denounce evil, more eager than most to act for human betterment. For all that, his was a human life. That is its inspiration to us humans. And somehow through the centuries some people have seen, behind the lie of the golden cross, his real life and his real death, and have been moved to follow his way of bettering, or of trying in their own way to better the world. That trial, as Jesus attempted it, brought him to his end. It brought him to prison, to torture, and at last to the instrument of capital punishment of his day. It brought him to the cross. Not so quick, not so kind in lethal action as our electricity or gas but in its own way it effected the criminal brand upon its victims just as concisely. So it was that Jesus who tried to make the world better died on a cross between two thieves at the hands of society, which frequently fails to distinguish between its worst and its best members.

And what does that cross mean to liberals in religion? Not the gilded cross, now! Not the sacramental symbol! Not the magic springboard to heaven! What does the real cross, the true cross, the plain rude wooden cross, the convict's cross, upon which the man Jesus died, what does *that* cross mean to liberals? I consider it, first of all, a symbol of the inevitable opposition with which the majority always attempts to bludgeon the minority into submission and silence. Cross, firing squad, electric chair, hanging, torture chamber, third degree, "lose your job," "lose the election," jailed, ostracized, smeared, these are methods of enforcing conformity. Frequently the person who tries to change mere goodness into better meets with resentment and sometimes with persecution. The degree of opposition with which a liberal is met depends upon the degree in which he is understood as a worker for change, and the degree to which his society has been civilized. But the liberal always raises opposition. There will always be opposition to change for the better.

If you are a convinced liberal working in all phases of life for a better way you had better be prepared to face and to deal with opposition in any degree.

Deal with it with whatever efforts you can muster. Organization is the best weapon: the close-knit, dedicated group. Jesus had such a group. A church is such a group. I could not stand to speak for very long in a community were it not for the support a church gives me. You would not speak as freely nor as forcibly for your convictions were it not for your membership in a group. In the early 1930's the Nazis of Germany were picking off the liberals one by one. There was no solid organization among them to fight back. So, easily, they went down. In the late 1930's single nations were being picked off one by one by the Nazis. They had not learned that "ten men united in love can do, what ten thousand singly would fail in." They did not learn. They went down. Many individuals have not yet learned it. By themselves they think they are sufficient unto themselves. But there stands the wooden cross on Golgotha's hill. Plainly it says to all but fools: Organize, co-operate — or die! And even with a dedicated but small organization you may go down!

But more than this the cross means to me. Many people these days are asking a pertinent question. They want to know how it is possible, with evil rampant in personal and social life, that any better world can come to be? How can good come out of evil? Indeed how? The answer, even in theory, isn't easy. In practice it is even harder. But there is an answer! How have we come this far out of total savagery? Not by any magical grace from God, nor by way of a gilded cross. We have come this far out of savagery into humanity on the backs of those who were willing and able to carry their fellows along. Teachers, preachers, prophets, inventors, explorers, experimenters, did the job. The scouts, the crackpots, the advanced guard, the liberals, those who failed twice for every successful effort, yet, despite opposition and failure fought on sacrificially, and died searching the truer, advancing a better they knew was yet to be. On these backs have we moved ahead! Those who suffered the derision of the multitude for a new idea, those who risked persecution for an ethical improvement, those who died defending a right against majority suppression, all those — the thousands of faithful men and women in our history have purchased our world for us in personal sacrifice. The cross is their sign.

I know of no better symbol for liberals than the cross: the plain crossed sticks of splintery wood. Jesus died on the cross precisely because he was a liberal in his day. Liberals are like yeast to the dough, like ferment in the grape. They are the germ of progress. Without them society would perish in lethargy like a body without food. Yet never has society been without them. Always they come, the pioneers exploring the new, the prophets announcing the better, the liberals struggling for progress, giving themselves sacrificially. These are the mothering hearts of a better world. These in personal sacrifice belabor goodness out of evil. And that is why it comes. The world gets better because some people will risk ostracism for the better. It progresses because some saints are not afraid of being called sinners. Good comes out of evil because some people have taken up a cross, a wooden cross with not a golden glint on it, and in sacrifice will carry it to the end.

This is what the cross means to me. It is a warning that I must join my fellows on the road of life. It is an explanation of how the better comes to be. It is a rallying symbol for those who would make the better.

But more. It is a goad to a comfortable life. It is shame upon all cowardice. It is the resolution of many doubts. It is an inspiration to labor.

The cross stands clearly as a threat of death to all those who would take up the burden of change. Yet it symbolizes also something beyond. They hung Jesus on a cross to be rid of him and all he taught. Yet that cross did not kill the thing he was, and meant, and taught. We have his teachings with us yet. There are times when, somehow, I think I can hear him, still preaching from the cross that failed to kill the dedicated spirit of the man.

Listen, you liberals! Maybe you can hear it too. Listen: "Take up your cross and follow me!"

XVI

WHEN THE ATOM BOMB FALLS

"The quest for a substitute for God (has) ended suddenly. The substitute turned up. And who do you suppose it was? It was man himself, stealing God's stuff."

So declares E. B. White in his potent little book of collected editorials called *The Wild Flag*. He suggests that man now substitutes for God because he has learned the secret of the atom. No longer must he use clumsy machinery in his attempts to change one form of energy into another, coal into heat and heat into steam and steam at last in locomotion or electricity. Now, after his years of questing and puzzling and figuring and inventing, scientific men have plumbed a mystery, bared an atomic universe to human view, and with avid skill use the source of energy as energy itself.

Conversion of energy to human use is now an old-fashioned idea, the employment of which left the universe no poorer than before; no smaller than before. But in atomic fission, the universe itself is whittled away, leaving not even the shiny chips of the whittler's knife to show for it. In old-fashioned methods of converting energy, humans changed the form of the universe a little bit each time they ran a train, lighted a light, or shot a gun. Now it is in man's power not only to change the form of nature, but literally and actually to use up the very stuff out of which energy flows. Relatively, the old method is slow, cumbersome, tiresome, inefficient.

Atom smashing scientists are insisting that within a generation a piece of cardboard the size of a match cover will, if literally destroyed, give enough energy to drive a passenger train four times around the world. Now don't ask me where they are going to lay the tracks for that train. I don't know. But I do know that merely converting a match cover into flame and the flame into steam and the steam into locomotion would hardly move a toy train along one section of its track in your living room. Manipulating a conversion of power was our old-fashioned, and now inefficient, way. Actually using up, destroying energy for our use, is the new version, and within a generation may be the new way.

Atomic fission promises mankind an almost limitless supply of cheap energy. One scientist, speaking of the possibilities of releasing the potential energy of common elements, has suggested that smashing the atom in one pound of water might very well heat one hundred million tons of water from the freezing to the boiling point. And smashing to pieces the atoms in a single breath of air might create enough energy to drive an airplane motor steadily for a year. A handful of snow, obliterated forever in atomic fission, might in the obliteration heat an apartment house through a long winter.

We may be afraid of using up the world supply of oil or coal. Few people, at least so far, have seriously believed that we could ever be piggish enough to use up the whole universe under our feet, and over our heads, and all about us. Using up the universe is so much more efficient than converting one form of energy into another for our use that we need not worry about it. We can bask content in our new-found god-like powers and by waiting for a few years — behold, we will be living under new heavens in a new earth, where tears will flow only for joy, and sweat and sorrow will have fled away. Man will be God, then, and all the world a paradise.

But will man, with his world-shaking, mind-pro-voking discovery of atomic energy, turn out to be so benign, so beneficent, so kindly a God toward himself and his fellows? That it is possible he may do so I have no doubt. That it is our great challenge in this atomic age to make these fine dreams a reality seems to me clear and inescapable. But that mankind must necessarily act the part of a good and creative God in his knowledge of atomic fission and its use is far from a foregone conclusion. More and more of us are coming to the conclusion that atomic energy is rapidly becoming both our greatest human hope and our gravest human fear.

Atomic energy within a generation may mean a better life or a horrible death for the greater part of the human race. If the godlike explorations of the mind of man have led him to this secret of atomic fire, how do we know that in the end mankind will not turn out to be a vengeful, angry, self-destructive God in the pattern of other gods we have known? We don't know! Atomic energy was discovered not by men in search of creative improvement of the human race, it was discovered by men in vigorous seeking after a more comprehensive way of mass destruction. Very recently some of those same men formed the Emergency Committee of Atomic Scientists, and set out to raise a million dollars to start a program of education, seeking "through enlightenment to prevent able statesmen from being hampered in their work by antiquated notions and prejudices." And then, to let no grass grow under the feet of their educational program, they issued the following statement, which contains hardly a suggestion of hope for a brave new world:

> "1. Atomic bombs can now be made cheaply and in large number. They will become more destructive.
> 2. There is no military defense against atomic bombs and none is to be expected.
> 3. Other nations can rediscover our secret processes by themselves.
> 4. Preparedness against atomic war is futile, and if attempted, will ruin the structure of our social order.
> 5. If war breaks out atomic bombs will be used, and they will surely destroy our civilization.
> 6. There is no solution to this problem except international control of atomic energy and, ultimately, the elimination of war."

Clearly, then, the superintelligences who discovered atomic fission and then manufactured the atomic bomb see no hope for the survival of the present civilization, let alone an improvement of it, unless effective international control of atomic energy is realized, which means the yielding of large areas of national sovereignty to an effective world government for the abolishment of world war.

If we are to survive as civilized peoples we must take these radical steps toward world integration and improvement. If we do not, the atom bombs will fall. New bombs, larger bombs, more bombs, the bombs of many nations who even now are working for the secret and sooner or later will find it. And when the atom bomb falls, with it falls civilization! So declare the atomic scientists.

In the December issue of *Harper's Magazine,* a storyteller suggests that a Godlike mind, human or otherwise, is weighing civilization in the scales to determine if civilization is worth saving from atomic disintegraton. And Pat. Frank, in the best-selling novel, *Mr. Adam,* lampoons our insane power-madness in the face of imminent death, leaving it a little dark whether mankind is worth saving or not.

For myself, I have no such cynical doubts. Civilization is worth saving. And, moreover, at no time in human history have people had a greater right to hope for betterment and a greater incentive to work for improvement. On the positive side, our work is clearly cut out for us: to create a world government, world law, world court, world police force, outlawing atomic energy for human destruction, abolishing war, and controlling atomic energy for creative use in all the world. Here is the practical program; practical because necessary for survival. And anything else, any less ambitious goal, the purest kind of impractical prudence, because for once at least in history, radical idealism is practical necessity for survival. The alternative is a falling rain of atomic bombs.

There is no substitute for this list of necessities. Oratorical trickery will not prevent the bombs falling. Propaganda will not stop it, and may indeed hasten it. The biggest army will not stop the bomb. A two-ocean navy may bring that fall sooner, rather than later. Treaties between nations will not prevent atomic bombing. Only world government, with teeth in it, will furnish world law, a universal world "justice," and the outlawing of the destructive war use of atomic energy. World government is the positive, practical goal all peoples of intelligence and courage and good will will work for in the years ahead. Yet, for all our working to have it otherwise, the atom bomb may fall. Many of us worked for years to prevent the last war's destructive bombing. And yet, it came. And so it may be with the atom bomb. One need not be cynical in working for the better to be prepared for defeat along the way.

And if that statement sends ice down your back, I can only say I'd rather, in the name of vital, realistic religion, have you prepared now against possible failure than to have you shocked into surprised neuroticism some years hence. I know people are talking about "when the atom bomb falls." Haunted eyes have looked across smoky tables for many weeks past, speculating about "when the bomb will fall." I know that the farm real-estate market has picked up as a result of talk of what will happen in our cities "when the atom bomb falls." I know that many people are already minor neurotics, worrying about the falling atom bomb. When the atom bomb falls! When the atom bomb falls! When the atom bomb falls! It echoes through living rooms and lecture halls and over bar tables and on the quiet beach like the tragic refrain of some chorus in a Greek tragedy — "when the atom bomb falls!"

Well, the atom bomb has already fallen. It fell on Hiroshima. Where before it had taken two hundred seventy-nine planes dropping thousands of bombs to kill five thousand three hundred people per square mile in a modern city, one plane, dropping one bomb, was shown at Hiroshima to be able to kill fifteen thousand people per square mile. The atom bomb has already fallen on Nagasaki, with even more startling results. There one bomb killed almost forty thousand in two square miles; twenty thousand people per square mile! You have doubtless read about those bombings in Japan in the calm report of John Hersey. When the atom bomb drops, the grim reaper walks through industrial cities cutting wide swaths of death with inexorable impartiality in his choice of youths and aged, boys and girls, husbands and wives.

To have read John Hersey's account is to feel the bomb falling all over again. The fact is, that for imaginative and for informed minds, the atom bomb has already fallen with a sickening, prolonged explosion in their hearts. And that's why there are distracted faces, haunted eyes, and talk over the bar tables. And that's why city folks, for the first time in the history of America, are seeing new value in farm life.

Yes, at Hiroshima and Nagasaki and in all our hearts, the atom bomb has already fallen. We know its destructive power. We know that our job is cut out for us, our practical job, the job of doing all we can to advance world law, world government, for all our welfare.

But suppose, despite our best efforts, the atom bomb falls on these shores. Suppose the goal of world peace controlled by international law was too high a goal and the time to achieve it too short. Suppose the atom bomb falls on the United States. One sterner question: when the atom bomb falls, suppose it falls on us and our families and our friends, and destroys us and our civilization!

How shall we act, if it really is to happen? How shall we act *now?* How shall we act between now and then? Not fifteen or twenty or thirty years from now, but now—I am asking you to stare death in the face, to face the end of civilization. And I pose this question: if this ghastly end be ours, and that of our civilization, "How shall we act meantime? How shall we act, beginning now?"

Perhaps you find that a startling question. Maybe you think that it is sordid. Possibly you think it a shocking new question, posed by a new discovery. Let me reassure you. It is an old, old question, which every religion worth its salt has always sought to answer. Plato's dialogues abound with the question, though, of course, no human death in his day was caused by atom bombs. Plato might have put the question: "What will you do with your life?" And Aristotle continued asking the question: "What ends are worthy the service of a wise man?" And Jesus asked of what avail it was to gain the whole world and lose one's own significance. And Marcus Aurelius and Buddha and many more have suggested that a person has not started to live thoughtfully until he faces the fact that some day he will not live at all!

You are going to die! You knew it all the time. And even if we achieve a world order and outlaw the atom bomb and it never falls on you, or never falls on anybody, a coconut may. Or you may fall in your bath; or a motorcar, or a disease, or old age will take your life at last. And how will you live, meantime? You see, atom bomb or coconut, it is the identical question that foresighted people face. And we can add, that our children, sooner or later, will also die, and so also will our civilization. How to live before you die is an old, old question.

I think the way to live between now and eventual death is first of all to realize that each of us is possessed of a treasure. That treasure is life itself; awareness, consciousness, and an ability to think, to love, to dream up goals for action, to strive toward their completion, to rest, to be recreated, to contemplate, to learn to be a part of life and other lives, yet also in other moments to exist in the mind as apart from all others.

Life is the gift. Life is the miracle. And if you have it in you to appreciate the gift and to wonder mightily in your heart at the miracle of life, I think you will not find it too difficult to accept the plain and simple fact of death. I believe much more about life and more about death than I have time now to say. But these few things I do want to say. Life is a miracle, and death is a fact. And to use that miracle for all it is worth of loving, striving, understanding, studying and playing, trying, searching, and in the whole process to enjoy the moments of creativity as they fleet by, is to be worthy of the miracle. Sorrow, sadness, defeat and death at the end of life are the salt of life which gives life its flavor. I do not want to exist on salt. But I find myself unable to think about existing in life without it. No person, I think, can enjoy more than he has suffered. And though neither joy nor sorrow are the end of life, the creative richness of life is more real and vital because both pain and pleasure are in it. And were a personal God to judge me at any moment of my life, I think I would have to plead guilty to enjoying more than enough fine moments in life to compensate for its hells.

How should we live then, between birth and death, between now and the falling atom bomb, if, despite our best efforts, it does fall? Why, I think we should live as if life were sacred, as if life were a responsibility, as if life were a constant attempt to change fearing into trusting, hating into loving. We should live in the persistent attempt to displace power-madness with security of body and spirit. We should live striving to change a warring world into a peaceful world. And our joy in living ought to come to us and will come to us, not because we succeed, nor because we fail. Joy in life — creative joy — is the accompaniment of creatively trying to reach toward goals we set for ourselves. Atom bomb, or no atom bomb, whether it falls, or whether it doesn't fall, I am going to have fun. I am going to have fun trying to see what my little brain and these feeble hands can do to turn this instrument of destruction into creative use for all mankind.

I will sweat and groan maybe; I will yelp or shout sometimes; I shall, despite myself, think of failure or success sometimes; but I will have some real creative pain, pleasure, thrill, in trying to change world chaos into world government. And so far as I can understand it at the moment, the pain, pleasure, thrill of trying anything you think worth-while is the chiefest way of honoring the miracle of your own life-breathing organism. The coming of death, the falling or not falling of a bomb is not the most important thing. The most important thing is your life, interrelated and in some real sense inseparable from other lives: to try to make it creative for all it is worth.

To try! Success and failure have our minds in their clutches in our culture to such an extent that we worry ourselves to an early grave, thinking of them. I am convinced some of the orientals had a better way. In the Bhagavad-Gita we are instructed to perform our duties in action but "without attachment." As far as I can make out, this means: try to do what you believe in, but don't stay awake all night in your bed, where you should be at rest, worrying the long night through about whether, in the world's eyes, you are going to succeed or fail in your trying.

Have fun trying. Try because it's right, because it's better. Try because you ought to try. And when you are worn out with the creative thrill of trying, then go off and enjoy a good meal. Listen to music. Read a book. Play chess. Sail a boat. Go fishing. Have a talk with your friend. Make love to your mate. Play with the children. Lie in the sun. Dream up, lazily, objectively, another angle for tomorrow's trying. But for the sake of the God that may be in you, don't lie stiff and tense on your couch, doubting your personal ability to create a world government in time to keep that devil of a bomb from dropping. Sinner — oh Sinner! Where will you stand in that great day, if man, turned self-destructive god, should choose to rain down atomic fire?

Well, Walt Whitman has one good answer. Says old Walt:

"O, to die advancing on!
Are there some of us to droop and die? Has
    the hour come?
Then upon the march we fittest die!"

When the atom bomb falls, if it does fall on us, despite the best efforts of thousands of earnest men and women to prevent it, then this sinner, who will share in the general judgment of that day, will, I hope, be in the study at home, whacking out in hot creative licks the words of next Sunday's sermon. Or, better still, I'd like to be with you in the creative act of preaching that sermon, urging myself and you to keep on trying, to joy with our lives — trying! Or, if that bomb should fall on Monday, I hope there will not be such a press of consultations or weddings as to prevent this sinner from just plain "going fishing." That's a relaxing thing to do after a hard day's work. Whenever it happens, for me or for you, I rather like to think that somebody will be just plain "fishing" on some quiet, sparkling, sunlit inlet, come judgment day.

Should our culture go down with the falling atom bombs, a fishing boat ought to be as good a place as any to begin to try to start all over again. Wasn't Adam himself started off on a river bank?